To Marsha & Buddy
See page 199
Enjoy
Leslie Friedman

INCARCERATED AT AGE 7

Holocaust Memoirs
by Leslie Friedman

Edited by
Azriela Jaffe

Preface

My story is unusual.

How many people can report being imprisoned as a seven year old?

Millions of children of that age were murdered in the crematoriums. The only children who survived were those in hiding, many living out their young years in bunkers and straw piles in barns, waiting for the war to end. Even fewer children can report that they were captured and put into a prison and survived.

Holocaust survivors who are still alive to tell their story are typically in their late eighties and nineties, if they entered into the concentration camps as young adults, and were spared gassing because they were capable of working.

But here I am, with a unique story to tell in my late seventies. I managed to avoid concentration camps, so I was granted the good fortune to go on to live a wonderful life. But that doesn't mean I emerged unscathed. Such a frightening experience did get imbedded in my psyche and showed its ugliness from time to time in my adult life. Without question, losing my mother, who was murdered by the Nazis, shaped my life in ways known, and unknown.

I am, indeed, a Holocaust survivor, even if my story is quite different.

As you read my story, you will hear of my gratitude for the opportunities provided me by many loving people who reached out a hand to me, as a young immigrant arriving in America, and throughout my high school, college, and professional years. Without question, in my mother's absence, my father, stepmother, younger brother, in-laws, aunts and uncles, and close friends were the village that helped to raise me.

And then, there is Barbara. She deserves her own paragraph – really, her own book! Words are insufficient to describe how she has been my rock, and close partner in life for really, my entire adult life. Everything I enjoy in my life I can ascribe to being with her. When I was down, she lifted me up. When I was up, she shared those good times with me. I pray to G-d that we have many more good years together in health, to enjoy our beautiful family together.

Acknowledgements

The writing of my autobiography would never have happened had not my son Doug presented me with a tape recorder and an outline back in November 2014. He requested that he and his siblings would like to know what I went through during the war and he asked me to put my thoughts down on paper so it wouldn't be forgotten after my passing.

Doug also put me in touch with Azriela Jaffe, my memoirist, who also provided me with the tools to be able to write and publish this book. Without those two individuals this book would never have come to be.

My whole family has been an inspiration to me over time, which enabled me to write about them with pleasure. I thank them for who they are and how they reflect my being.

Above all I want to thank my wife who has been my backbone throughout our life together, including some ups and downs created by illness that derived from my early childhood imprisonment and the tragic murder of my mother by the Nazis. No matter what I suffered, or why, she never left my side.

Over the years I have run into many good people, including teachers friends and clients from whom I learned much. My thanks goes out to everyone who has touched my life over several decades.

Les Friedman

Table of Contents

CHAPTER 1

My Family of Origin

My Father's Family

My paternal grandfather, Morris Friedman and grandmother, Rose Friedman lived in a small town, *Krompachy*, Czechoslovakia, which was a town of eight thousand, twenty percent Jewish. My grandfather was a prominent member of the Jewish community, serving as both a *shochet* and a cantor. Together, with my grandmother, they raised a large family of eleven children - five boys and six girls, with my father in the middle of the pack.

I never met my grandmother, as she passed away before I was born. I am told that my grandmother was a very slight woman under five feet tall. It couldn't have been easy to give birth to eleven children, (including one set of twins), for such a petite woman.

My grandfather Morris and the youngest daughter Gita, the only unmarried daughter, immigrated to the United States after my grandmother passed away, so he could make a better living and send money home to care for the rest of the children. My father was at this time about twenty years old. My grandfather was a religious man with a large beard and he secured a job in Pennsylvania as a *shochet* and a cantor who performed for the holidays and anytime anyone needed to pray before a congregation. He would travel with his pots and pans and his instruments for doing the chicken killing to many small towns in Pennsylvania. The pots and pans that he carried were the same pots and pans he used to cook for himself in!

Of eight children who went through the Holocaust, only three survived, my father being one of them, along with my Uncle Jose, and my Aunt Irene.

This is a brief account of the horrific loss to my father's family from the Nazi regime:

Of my eleven aunts and uncles:

1. Jose, a widower and his two sons and a daughter survived a pilgrimage to Russia, taking Torahs with him for their safekeeping.
2. Haskel died as a child.
3. Margit, one of the twins, immigrated to America before the war. She lived in Pennsylvania, and had a daughter and son who will be described later in the book.
4. Fanny, the other twin, lived in Prague perished in the Holocaust with her husband and two girls and one boy.
5. Hermine lived in Prague, and she perished with her husband and two children in the Holocaust.
6. Yolan lived in *Michalovce* with her husband and one son; they perished in the Holocaust.
7. Mendel my father survived! His story is told in more detail in this memoir.
8. Irena survived the Holocaust with her husband and two children; details of their survival are detailed in the book.

9. Lazer immigrated to Israel before the war. He married in Israel and had three children. Lazer and his wife are deceased but his children and grandchildren are living in Israel. We have visited all of them when we were in Israel as I mention later in the book.
10. Gita perished in the Holocaust with my grandfather.
11. Petu perished in the Holocaust.

My Father

My father, Emanuel, was born on January 24, 1907 in *Krompachy*, Czechoslovakia. My father was 5' 7", with slender build, and wore glasses and a Hitler type mustache until it was not fashionable for Jews to adorn such a mustache. My father was very strong and agile; I once saw him play soccer and was very impressed by how fast he was. He was a very honest man who couldn't tell a lie. He was very religious and liked to pray on the pulpit. When he did, the congregation appreciated his expressive voice.

During his teens he broke his nose when he fell ice skating. He never went to a doctor and when his nose healed, he ended up with a nose like Dick Tracy, the cartoon character, instead of the hooknose that he probably would've had.

My father was a very smart man, but not a well-educated man by secular standards. He went to elementary school in his town and finished his education at a yeshiva in a nearby city where he boarded. He never attended high school. When he graduated from the yeshiva at the age of fourteen, it was customary for the boys in the family to get jobs and help their parents to pay the bills, especially in large families of eleven children without a mother to care for them. He worked in stores doing odd jobs until his older brother Jose opened a general store in a nearby city. Then he left home and went to work for his brother.

My father and his sister Irena spent the war years together and survived. My father's brother Jose, who was a *gabbai* at his synagogue, rescued the Torahs from his temple and brought them with his family on a pilgrimage to Russia, where he and his family survived. Jose, who was widowed since before the war, eventually immigrated to Australia with his two sons, where his daughter was living. After the war, Jose's daughter married a man from Australia and moved there. Barb and I never made it to Australia to see this part of the family.

My aunt Irena and her children moved back and forth between family in Belgium and Czechoslovakia. She was not able to get a visa to come to America once the communists took over Czechoslovakia. Eventually she succumbed to grief from the loss of her husband right after the war ended and her life was very bitter. She died in 1957 and left two teenage children, Ervin and Edith (Edit), to fend for themselves. I admire how Ervin took care of Edith, in that communist world they lived in before they left for America in 1958, sponsored by their father's brother, Uncle Nathan Grunberger.

Edith went to live with her Uncle Nathan in New York when she was fifteen and visited with us in Cleveland that summer when she arrived. After finishing school she met an Israeli boy in New York and they were married and Immigrated to Israel, where they lived and raised two boys and a girl. Shortly after Ervin came to the United States he went into the Army. I was not in contact with him initially but later when he moved to Los Angeles we met him at my father's house, as he also moved out there, which I will discuss later. Since than Ervin and I have had many get togethers in many places and a whole lot of telephone conversations.

My Mother's Family

My mother, Olga was born in 1912. As a teen, she fell off of a wagon and suffered some permanent damage to her leg, resulting in a limp for the rest of her days. She was about 5' 3", medium build, with a kind, affectionate and very likable personality. I was very young when I lost her so my memories of her are very faint. But I do remember that she was always taking care of me and I seemed to preoccupy most of her time. My aunts tell me that she was one of the siblings who was the most friendly, good hearted and well liked. She was religious to the point of keeping kosher and the Sabbath but a little more relaxed than my father and his family, who were sterner about religious matters.

On my mother's side the Rosner family lived in *Satoraljaujhely*, Hungary. (Yes, that's a mouthful and most Americans have no clue how to pronounce it!) My mother was one of seven siblings - one boy, Mano and six girls: Terka, Ila, Honor, Bosze, Olga, Mancy.

I never knew my maternal grandfather Isidor since he passed away before I was born. Of the seven children, only Mano and my mother remained in Hungary. The rest immigrated before the war, escaping the death sentence of the Holocaust. Honor immigrated to Israel, and the other four sisters, Terka, Ila, Bosze, and Mancy immigrated to the United States. They married, and had one child each except for Bosze who never had a child. Bosze brought us to United States and I tell that story later in this memoir.

Tragically, my mother, her brother, Mano, and her mother, my grandmother, were murdered in the Holocaust.

Rosner family, 1934
My mother is left front
2 sisters missing

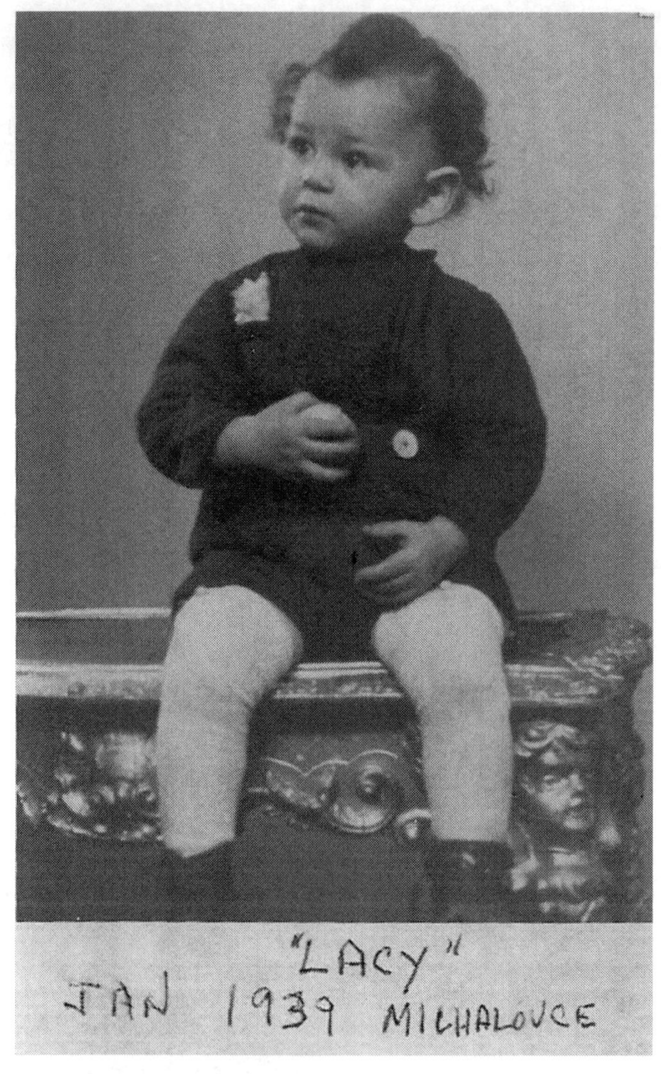

1939, three years old

CHAPTER 2

My Parents and My Birth

On February 9 1935, when my father was twenty-eight years old and my mother was age twenty-three, my mother and father exchanged wedding vows under the chuppah.

February 9, 1935.
My mother and father

My parents' families were related and a shidduch was made. The wedding was in my mother's hometown *Satoraljaujhely*.

I was born to them on July 8 1936, their first child.

My given legal name was "Lazlo" in Hungarian, but my nickname was Laci.[1] I

[1] When we moved to Czechoslovakia my legal name was changed to Ladislav, and

My grandma's house where I was born, photo taken in 1989

was born in my grandmother's house where we were living, in the small town of *Satoraljaujhely*. We lived there until I was six months old and then we moved to *Michalovce*, Czechoslovakia, which was just over the Hungarian border, and less than fifteen miles from where I was born. (I returned to this house under adverse conditions when World War II started.)

My home town

Both *Michalovce* and *Satoraljaujhely* were cities that had a Jewish presence.

when we immigrated to America, my cousin, somewhat fluent in English, decided that I should be called Ladislaus. (My father turned scrap gold into a pinky ring made for me with that name inscribed. Unfortunately, when I was in my teens I lost the ring while swimming in a pool.) My Aunt Bosze gave me a new name of Leslie since she did not think Ladislaus was proper for living in America. My last name, Friedman, is also not the original name I was born with, because my birth certificate from Hungary, which I acquired when I applied for social security in America, shows that my given name was spelled "Friedmann."

Michalovce had a population of about thirty thousand, of which forty percent was Jewish. The town had several synagogues and its own Jewish school system.

Satoraljaujhely, (most often referred to as *Ujhel* because of its ungodly spelling) was much smaller than *Michalovce* with about a 10,000 population of which less than 205 families were Jewish. One could contrast the two cities also as *Michalovce* being more Orthodox and *Ujhel* leaning more to Conservative.

In *Michalovce* the main street was lined with stores and commercial buildings. Between these buildings there were entrances to the back of the buildings where there were residences, one of which we occupied.

My parents slept in the master bedroom and I slept in a very small bedroom next to it, more like a walk-in-closet! The house also had a kitchen and dining area and the couch we sat on was actually located in my parents' bedroom. We accessed running water only in the kitchen, from a pump in the sink and were relied on an outhouse in the backyard. There also was a shed where we stored split wood for the ceramic stove in the bedroom that heated the whole house. In the winter my parents would put bricks in the furnace which when heated they would wrap in towel and put them at our feet to keep us warm at night.

My mother and me

In this new town my dad established a gas station and a delivery business with a truck provided him by my mother's family when he got married. My dad did not drive, so he hired a driver and he would make the arrangements for deliveries. He hired workers to service the cars at the gas station, and he was the inside person. I have an early memory of pedaling around the gas station in a new blue pedal car that I was gifted with when I was four years old.

My mother walked me to school to attend kindergarten when I turned five.

Ervin (on left) and I going to Kindergarten, 1941

In my young childhood, I enjoyed relatively good days, even though there was a lot of anti-Semitic activity all around us. We attended Jewish schools run by teachers and rabbis who were totally separated from the Gentiles who had their own school system. To discipline us the rabbis would use a stick to hit us on our palms, or the tips of our fingers. We were very afraid of this punishment so it was very effective. There was a large yard where we played soccer and other games. We actually invented the hula-hoop when I was just a kid - we used to take a wooden circle like a hula-hoop and run behind it and hit it with a stick.

Very often we traveled back across the border to where my grandma lived and where I was born. My mother and I visited my grandma and my uncle Mano who was a single schoolteacher and lived with my grandmother. I remember my uncle putting me on top of a wardrobe that would make me laugh. When I was three or four he would take me in the backyard and we would throw the fruit that had fallen from the trees. The back yard had many fruit trees like an orchard. This was one of the houses my grandma owned. She owned two other homes in this area - one had stables in the back and

1938, my Mother, me, Aunt Honor

the other had a bakery in the front. Most of both homes were rented as residences.

In 1938 my aunt Honor, on her way to Israel from the United States, came to visit her mother and family. It was summertime and we spent time in the back yard in bathing suits. I have several pictures of my mother, grandmother, aunt Honor, and me, from this event, which I include in this memoir.

My early childhood was wonderful. I share with you a long-ago memory still with me that really captures the innocence and delight of my childhood before the Nazis stole it away.

The train in *Shatoraljaujhely* went down the Main Street for local transportation. At the end of the street there was a turn around where the train engineers would manually turn the single car train around and head back. I used to watch them turn the train around. Who needed toys and television and electronic gadgets? Life was simple, and fun!

1938, me and my grandmother

I had a loving mother and father who provided all my needs. I remember my mother walking me in the stroller. When a stranger would look at me, my mother, being superstitious, would take a glass of water when she got home and put a lump of coal in it to ward off bad spirits. She would also make me wear a piece of garlic on a string around my neck. Most days my mom and I would have a snack in the kitchen consisting of freshly baked bread and butter with scallions or bread with *schmaltz* and *grivenes*, which my mom would prepare by frying chicken fat.

I wish I could tell you more about my mother but I was seven years old when I last saw her, and seven decades later, the fact that I have any lingering memories of her at all is a testimony to the bond we shared, and the magnitude of my loss.

Me, watering the garden

Aunt Honor, my mother and me

Aunt Honor and me, 1938

Uncle's store in Preshove, Czech. Note two "N's" at the end of the name.

Cousin Erwin's parents

1945, Ervin and his sister. I spent the war years with him

Aunt Mancy, my mother and me

The prison gate

CHAPTER 3

My Childhood Escape

My grandfather and his youngest daughter of eleven children, Gita, left the United States in 1938, returning to Czechoslovakia because he thought the family needed him. This turned out to be a tragic decision for my grandfather.

When I was in first grade, the Nazis took control of our region, and life became very difficult for my family and the Jews in our community. Initially, we did not have German soldiers in our midst. The Germans would use the local Czechoslovakian police and give them orders to hinder and hurt the Jews. My family had to start wearing a yellow star on our clothing.

Next, the Czechoslovakian government conscripted my father into labor camp. One day I saw my father in the house when he was supposed to be in labor camp. My mother tried to convince me that I did not see him. Later I found out that he had escaped from the labor camp and was hiding in the attic of our house. He remained in hiding and never went back to the labor camp until we ran to the remote woods to hide.

Soon the Nazis began to take the older people and gypsies and put them into cattle cars for transporting them to unknown parts. My grandfather was selected for the transport. My aunt Gita would not leave my grandfather when they came for him and I am sure she came to the same fate as he did. At the time my grandfather was living with us, as he moved around between his children. His eyesight was failing and he would put his hand on my shoulder so I could lead him to where he wanted to go. Besides his failing eyesight, he also had high blood pressure, which was being treated by having leaches put on his back that would suck out the blood and reduce blood pressure (or so it was told.) I saw this taking place when it was his turn to stay with us. It was quite gruesome to see. For the most part my grandfather would sit on the side of the house on a small porch and just twiddle his thumbs for what seemed like hours.

Meanwhile, the Nazis were making daily life for the Jews very bad. My mother was in contact with her mother in *Satoraljaujhely*, Hungary. My mother was afraid that I would be taken away, like my father was. She decided to send me to stay by my grandmother.

Arrangements were made so that I would cross the border with some paid guides who did this for money all the time, usually helping women and children. My group had about six children and about the same number of women, not necessarily related. In my group there was one mother with two of her daughters who happened to be from my hometown.

Unfortunately at this crossing we were not lucky. The border guards stopped us, just after we crossed the river in a small boat. I was told to put my legs in the water and hold unto the inside of the boat with my arms and chest while it was crossing the river, so there was room for everyone on the rowboat. The river was like a canal about thirty yards wide and it did not take long. It seemed kind of adventuresome at first.

When we got up to the other side it was dark and we heard whistles blowing. The man transporting us told us to lie on the ground quietly and that he would be back for us. We laid there in the mud waiting for our guides to return, which took them what seemed to be a very long time, perhaps over a half hour. All the time I was wet and frightened. I became even more terrified when out of the darkness came uniformed police with dogs, blowing their whistles and pointing their guns at us!

The border guards took us by wagon to a small village where there was a prison occupied mainly by women and children. Most of the prisoners had a friend or relative with them, but I was alone. Fortunately, I was with the woman and her two daughters from my hometown and she reached out to me like a mother and gave me comfort.

The prison was more like an institution than a jail – similar to a nursing home. There were no bars on the windows. It consisted of many individual rooms and lot of common areas where everyone would mingle, and large dining areas where we ate okay food. We wore our own clothes and I remember the women wearing print peasant dresses with some kind of head covering.

I was imprisoned for about a month. We were not permitted to go outdoors. I remember playing indoor games, feeling frightened, bored, confined, and longing for my parents. I don't remember making any friends - just the mother and her two daughters from my hometown. They fed us enough; we weren't hungry.

One morning, a prison guard came to get me. He took me out of the prison and to an office where my uncle Mano, my mother's brother, was waiting for me to take me to my grandmother's house. I found out later that my uncle had paid off the police to get my release.[1]

I was so happy to see my uncle since he always was very nice to me and played with me a lot when I was smaller. I also remember

[1] In 1989 I went back to visit the prison, which I thought was in *Kishtarca*, but I found out when I got there it was actually in a sister city called *Noidtarca*. Unfortunately, I couldn't visit the prison since it was a Soviet training school and even pictures were not permitted. I did manage to take a couple pictures from a distance but I would have liked to have gone inside to see what I could recall from my imprisonment there as a boy.

The prison where I spent my seventh year

him helping me with my arithmetic tables. He was single, working as a schoolteacher, and living with my grandmother. He took me to my grandmother's house to live, so I was finally out of that prison.

When we got to my grandmother's house I was thrilled, as it was a place I frequently visited. I had no clue what was in store for us. It was just so good to be back with my family.

It wasn't long before the problems in Hungary escalated. The neighborhood that my grandmother's house was situated in was designated to be the ghetto area. Jewish families were being herded into our neighborhood. I still remember my grandmother standing on the street outside her house welcoming Jews who were coming down the street into her house. Then I saw the police putting up poles around this neighborhood and they hung barbed wire to fence in the ghetto designated area. When the prison was emptied, as were the ghettos, all these Jews were sent by transport to camps where most perished. My father told me that the mother and her two daughters who took such good care of me in the prison were taken, and killed in the camps. This made me feel very sad.

My grandmother was in touch with my mother, discussing if they thought it was best that I go back to my mother's house. They decided that I would be safer if I returned to my parents' home in *Michalovce.*

They made arrangements again with individuals to take me across the border. My uncle was aware of how serious the situation had become. Before I left, he showed me where he buried family jewelry in a pipe in the back yard of his house, in case something happened to him and my grandmother. None of the jewelry was ever found when we returned after the war to look for it.

My trip back home to Slovakia was another very unusual experience for a seven-year-old boy! On the return trip back to Slovakia a non-Jewish female guide who was accompanied by a boy, dressed me up in the Gardista Hitler youth uniform and put me into a hay wagon. Sometimes I also walked behind the wagon, accompanied by the guide or the boy. We crossed the river over a bridge that was guarded by police, but our group had papers and presented no problem. At the time, I remember feeling kind of proud to be wearing the uniform, as any seven-year-old boy would be. Later of course, I despised that uniform. The whole trip only took less than half a day, since my grandmother's house was less than five miles from the bridge that crossed the border, and the bridge to where my dad was working was less than ten miles from there.

The border crossing guides dropped me off at the railroad tracks near where my father was working. He had been forced to turn over his business, since all Jews were no longer permitted to own businesses. He elected to give his business to a gentile man named Miksa from the Czech Republic, because the Czechs were known to be less hostile to the Jews than the Slovaks. My father now worked for Miksa who was running my father's business. A big German Shepherd named Nero, who belonged to Miksa greeted me but I knew him and was friendly to me. I stayed with my father until quitting time. Then I walked about a half-mile home with him, eager to see my mother again.

We had this siddur in the bunker
from which my dad taught us to read and pray

CHAPTER 4

In Hiding

We continued wearing the yellow Star of David; every now and then we would hear of another family that was taken to parts unknown. At this point my father had two sisters with families and a brother with family still living in *Michalovce*. Every family was making decisions about what to do next.

My father's brother, Jose who was a very religious man, decided to take the Torahs from his temple and safeguard their keeping by moving towards Russia. One of my father's sister's Yolan and her family decided to stay in *Michalovce*. (They perished in the war). His other sister Irena and her family decided to stay with us on the plan that my father and his new Czech boss formulated.

We were to go by train to the mountains of Czechoslovakia, where my father's boss, Miksa had a company to construct railway bridges and tracks. My father had a job as a supervisor of the dynamite that was used in construction. This place was about a ten-hour railway ride away, to a very obscure farmhouse that he had picked for us to live with the farmer there. My dad made a very good decision in turning over his truck to Miksa. By traveling to this remote area, we were out of the major path of destruction and death for the Jews. My aunt Irena, her husband Emil and their two children, Ervin (who was eight months younger than me,) and Edith, who was just two years old, joined my mother, father, and me on this trek. We took with us only a couple of suitcases.

When we arrived at our destination we hired a wagon to the farmhouse where we would be staying. We stayed as a family in one large room in the farmhouse. This place was so desolate it was miles between farmhouses. When we arrived at the farm we played with the farmer's children, a boy and a girl, who had no idea we were Jewish, nor were they aware that harboring the Jews was a problem. I remember going fishing with the farmer's sons to a nearby brook and catching fish with a homemade hook and a stick. We caught fish and prepared them by scaling them and cooking them on an open fire like a shishkabob. That was the best fish I have ever eaten, then, or since!

The year was 1943. My father went to work every day. On some days his fellow workers would ask him to stay and have some drinks and my father was not a drinker so he would come home sick. When the farmers found out we were Jewish, and the Germans were coming close to our area, we had to make different arrangements, because my parents were frightened that they would be turned in.

Finding another place to live was no simple matter. Summer was arriving and rumors spread about how much trouble the farmers would get into if they were caught harboring the Jews. With the help of the farmer who originally housed us, a large underground area under the barn was excavated with a well-hidden passage from the second floor to the entrance. When it seemed dangerous, as Germans were nearby, we had to live in this underground bunker by day, and only come out at night. My aunt decided that my two-year-old cousin Edith should be placed with a gentile family, as she could not endure this type of living. They paid a farmer to keep her with them. She was blonde with blue eyes and easily passed for a gentile little girl. After the war my aunt and uncle went to pick Edith up from the farmhouse where they left her and to their dismay Edith did not recognize them and only wanted to stay with the farmer. Thankfully, after some coaxing she came with us.

My dad stopped working once it was known that he was Jewish. We had to stay in hiding. We paid the farmer money for food and for keeping quiet. Thank God for my Uncle Emil, who was a successful businessman and luckily was able to bring some money in one of those suitcases, so that we could exist.

We lived in and out of the bunker for about a year and a half. Try to imagine, if you will, what it must have been like for a young, active boy to spend hours and weeks in a hideout like this: The size was approximately 10' x 10', with earth walls and floor. The ceiling was made of rafters and wooden planking. The cows were standing above us on this planking, which created a terrible situation, since we had a hard time containing the seepage of the cows' urine. We didn't have plastic sheets so we just tried to plug up the holes with some rags that we found in this room. You can imagine the stench that came from cow urine, and we had no windows or doors to open to air out the area!

Four adults and two children slept on the floor, on bedding consisting mostly of quilts. When danger was lurking, which was often, we stayed in the bunker all day long and went out of the bunker only at night. At times, we were starving, as we could go many days with scarcely any food. Once in awhile the farmer would bring us a slab of bacon, but incredibly, even in with our desperate hunger, we couldn't bring ourselves to eat it, because it was so opposed to our religious practices that forbid eating pork. There was always temptation to eat the bacon but the farmer would bring us basic food to just get by.

Our stay in the bunker was mostly when danger lurked, such as when the Germans were getting close. Then, the farmer would alert us and we would go into hiding. While we were in the bunker we relied on bedding to keep us warm. We used candles and a kerosene lamp only occasionally, as we were afraid of the fumes. On some

Siddur, kaddish underscored

of these occasions my dad had a little *siddur* that I still possess from which he would try to teach Ervin and me how to pray.

My cousin Ervin, while living in New York, met Jack Joseph who told him that he visited us on the farm where we were hiding out; he had done business in the past with Ervin's father. Ervin gave him my phone number and when he called I had a long conversation with him. His original name was Jack Josefovitz and he was twenty years old when he came to our farmhouse from a neighboring farm miles away. My uncle Emil owed Jack's older brother some money from a business deal and Jack came to pick up the money. Being much older than me at that time, he was able to fill in many details for me. He shared that the farmer had a wife and two children, a boy and a girl, both slightly older than me. Jack also described the large, but crowded room that the three Friedmans and the three Grunbergers were living in. Jack remembers that Ervin and I were young and kept sheltered from too much knowledge of what was going on.

While we were hiding in the bunker, a Yugoslavian friendly air pilot was shot down and he parachuted from his plane near our hidden location. My dad and uncle discovered him, bandaged up his injured foot with rags, gave him supplies, and directed him to where he could meet up with friendly forces. My father would venture out of the farmhouse on occasion to find out what the situation of the war was. When the Russians were approaching our area, he saw some tremendous tragedies: he witnessed the Germans capturing some Russian soldiers, tying them to a plow and pulling the plow until they were dead. He also witnessed the Russians, in revenge, capturing some German soldiers and inhumanly beating and stabbing them with kitchen forks and knives.

After some months, the farmer told us that the Germans were getting very close and he was concerned about his and our safety. This situation prompted my dad and uncle to explore the woods, looking for a new hiding place. They found a large tree, which they excavated underneath to create a bunker that we could hide in if we needed to. Fortunately we didn't have to stay there and stayed nearer the farmhouse, underneath the excavated barn. In the daytime we would stay in this hideout and we would wander outside to stretch our legs and to take care of personal hygiene, which included using leaves for toilet paper. The weather often determined how long we could be outside.

Of course we had no medical, dental or any type of care for our well being and there were situations where we certainly needed such help. When we first arrived in this farm country they were harvesting some crops and using a machete to knock off the head of a cabbage. Thinking that I would do the same to be helpful, I managed to strike the machete into my hand. This mistake gave me a nasty cut which got infected; however my father and mother, with some home herbal remedies, were able to contain the infection and eventually it healed.

Tragically, while my mother was able to keep me from getting ill, the stress of our situation caused her to become so sick, no home remedy could save her. My father had no choice but to take her by wagon and train to the nearest hospital, hoping to save her life.

When my mother left the hideout, it was the last time I ever saw her. After the war ended, my father returned to the hospital, looking for information on my mother, and that's when he learned that she, and all of the patients, had been deported to concentration camp. We tried to trace where she went, hoping that somehow she had survived, but we were never able to find her.

The murder of my mother is a tragic loss I suffered from all of my life.

CHAPTER 5

Liberation

Our ordeal ended in March of 1945 when the Russians liberated our area. We went by wagon to the railway station where my uncle Emil, Aunt Irena, and cousins Ervin and Edith were waiting. Edith, a young girl who was picked up from the people she was staying with, tragically did not recognize her parents and had a hard time leaving the house she was staying at.

My father set out immediately for the hospital where he left my mother by wagon and foot, and the rest of us went by wagon to the railway station. The plan was, we were going to meet up with my father at the railway station. We did meet up with him and he told us the bad news about not finding my mother at the hospital and how everyone at the hospital was put on a transport and taken to concentration camps.

He of course hoped that she had somehow escaped from the hospital before this, or that she had survived the concentration camp if she was taken there. He told us we were going to look for her at my grandma's house, in case she returned there from the concentration camp.

We were very hopeful, and I'm sure, very nervous and sad at

even the thought that she had not survived.

We traveled by train, which happened to be carrying wounded Russian soldiers headed east, to my grandmother's house in Hungary. My father, Ervin and I got off the train as close to *Satoraljaujhely* as we could get, intending to walk the rest of the way. My aunt and uncle and Edit continued on the train until it got to *Michalovce*. We were heartbroken when we arrived at my grandmother's house, only to find it vacant. We went in the back yard to look for the valuables my uncle had hidden in the pipe, but the back yard had been excavated in many areas. I pointed to the area that my uncle had showed me but sadly, someone had gotten to it before us and there was no pipe anymore. What we found instead was certainly a big surprise - a large unexploded bomb sticking out of the ground in the backyard![1]

We were coming to terms with the devastating loss of my mother, although I'm sure my father still hoped he would find her somewhere. We left my grandmother's house and took the train to our home *Michalovce*, but the house was mostly destroyed, and we couldn't stay in the house. We moved in with Aunt Irena who had returned to *Michalovce* before us. Their house was not far away from our old house and it had running water throughout.[2]

My uncle Emil suffered while we were in the bunkers from an infected ear that affected his teeth as well. He had to go see a dentist and while on his way to a nearby town that had a dentist he got a ride on an open bed truck with barrels on the back of the truck where he also was riding. The truck had a flat tire and overturned and my uncle was thrown from the truck. Tragically, after all he had already suffered, one of the barrels hit him in the head and he died on the scene. His death was all the more tragic, to have survived the hardships of the Holocaust until liberation, only to be killed in such a senseless accident.

[1]Forty years later, when I went back to visit my grandma's house, the crater from the bomb was still there, but the bomb was not.

[2]Our previous house had only water in the kitchen, which you had to pump and the bathroom facility was an outhouse.

CHAPTER 6

Michalovce After the War

We tried to resume our lives after the war but it wasn't the same without having my mother there.

After my uncle passed away in the catastrophic accident, my aunt Irena and her son Erwin and daughter Edit continued living in the house with my father and me as one family. My father was the man of the house and my Aunt Irena did the chores of a mother. She was very distraught over the loss of her husband and when she received a letter from her brother-in-law from Brussels, Belgium, who sponsored her to go there, she decided to move there with her children. She stayed there a short while and then moved to Prague, because there were some problems with their visas.

Before Ervin left, he went to services every morning and every evening to say *kaddish* for his father. He became very knowledgeable and knew the services by heart. I was sorry that I never was able to say *kaddish* for my mother, as I never found out how, when, or where she died.[1]

[1] My father determined that my mother died around the second day of *Shavuot*,

When they left, I missed Ervin since we were always together, even though I was older and stronger. He had a way of teasing me, by calling me names like *Chunchu*, which meant "piggy" - that would get to me. Whenever Ervin or I did something bad that my father wanted to discipline us for, he would take off his belt and I would freeze and then Ervin would run around the dining room table, after which my father would say, "you have suffered enough," and then he would put the belt away.

Meanwhile, my father and I remained in *Michalovce*, where only a small semblance of Jews was left, because so many had perished in the Holocaust. My father and I continued to live in this house that was much more modern than any place I lived in before. Religious Jews must have previously occupied the house, since it had a built in *sukkah* in one of the back rooms. This room had a ceiling that would open up with a winch that would become the *sukkah* after covering the ceiling with special vines called *schach*. (When the ceiling was closed I stood on the roof and shot at targets below with an air rifle that I found.)

The river *Laborec* was nearby our home and we went swimming there as well as fishing. We employed the techniques that we had learned when we were at the farm making hooks and poles; however the results were not the same. The fish did not bite as well as they did when we were on the farm.

On the street that ran by the front of our house was a farmers market. The Bulgars (Bulgariens) were known for bringing excellent produce to sell in the market. One of the Bulgars who was right outside our house asked me to help him arrange some of the produce, which I did, and he gave me some tomatoes to take home as my

which I found out later was the date established by the Jewish community to honor those who perished on unknown dates. This proved to be a little bit of a situation for me since on the second day of *Shavuot*, the *Kaddish* is called *Rabunom Kaddish*, which is long and extremely difficult to say, like a tongue twister. When I went to Israel and made inquiries at *Yad Vashem* about my mother I found out her death was actually March of 1944, at the young age of only 31-years of age. From that point, I have said *Kaddish* for her on the second Thursday of March.

compensation. My father was very happy with this arrangement with the Bulgars, which lasted until I left the home.

My father found a job helping out on a bus traveling daily to Kosice and back. He was not a licensed driver, so he would assist the passengers and take tickets. This bus was often sold out and many days my father would give up his seat and sit on a stool, giving him and the driver some extra cash for selling his seat. The Friday trip was very difficult for my father since the bus would come back just before sundown. Sometime it was so close that he had to go to shul right from the bus, not even having time to go home first to clean up.

In addition to this job my dad and his cousin would do a little smuggling of yeast, as there was a shortage of this commodity in our parts. He and my cousin would go across the border to an adjacent country like Bulgaria and buy yeast and then bring it back to our parts and sell it on the black market. This journey was very dangerous, especially the border crossing when he was carrying all that yeast in backpacks that were heavy. When they couldn't get a wagon, he would have to walk many miles carrying this load on his back. There was harsh prison time if he was caught, so he gave it up in a short time. I'm sure it weighed heavily on him that I was already orphaned from my mother and it would be disastrous for me if he were imprisoned.

After the summer of 1945, in September, at the age of nine, I started my new school. It was so different than what I had been used to. We went to the same school as the gentiles and girls were included in our classes. The curriculum even included learning to speak Russian. After school the Jewish kids were to go their separate way to Hebrew classes in the old section where we used to have our classes, even though most of the classrooms were destroyed. Somehow we made do. After Hebrew classes we played soccer on the run down field by the semi-destroyed temple.

I remember one afternoon while playing soccer my father was watching me, all smiles, but when I came home he was angry because I was playing in the only shoes I had. We used a ball made from stockings and rags since we did not have a conventional ball.[2] We only had four or five players on each side, as that was all that was left of our guys. One of my good friends, Smilu Goldstein who was about a year older than me, was a very good soccer player.[3]

1947, Smilu on left. I am next to him, in Michalovce

We had one very dangerous situation playing within these semi-destroyed buildings. One day one of the boys found a whole bullet and the boys tried to detonate it by smashing it between two large stones. The bullet exploded and fortunately, only grazed one boy's thighs. We were all scared and never tried something like that again!

From 1945 – 1947, my father served as both my father and my mother and he tried not to be tough. I too, tried not to give him any trouble. I always behaved and listened to him. We did get a

[2] When I was leaving for America I told my soccer friends that I would send them a soccer ball from America. This never came to be, as I could not afford to buy a soccer ball and send it to them. We kids thought the money was just laying around in America and you could buy anything once you got there. Turned out, you had to work very hard for your money in America!

[3] I had the good fortune of meeting up with him in Brooklyn New York at his appliance store in 1996. After we met He sent me a picture of he and I and two of the other boys walking down Main Street of Michalovce in 1947, which I will always treasure, as there are not many pictures from those days since there were very few cameras.

housekeeper to help out with the cooking and cleaning. On occasion, my father would take me to a bar and I would sit next to him on a barstool. When my father would order a beer the bartender would bring the mug of beer and my father would let me sip the foam off the top.

In 1948 we found out that we would be going to America as our quota was coming up. My uncle Jose, my father's oldest brother, had a daughter Edith who was in her early twenties who spoke some English. She was trying to teach me some words. (This cousin was different than my aunt's daughter, Edith, who was only five years old at that time). Edith also translated my name from Ladislav to an Americanized version, Ladislaus. My father hearing this melted down a gold ring and made me pinky ring with the inscription *Ladislaus.* [4][5]

After a schoolboy incident, I was headed to Prague:

Even though the war was over, the surviving Jews and Gentiles did not get along. One day when the gentile boys were throwing rocks at us and calling us "dirty Jew", we retaliated and threw rocks back at them. One of the rocks knocked out the front tooth of one

Charles bridge in Prague, Hebrew letters on statuette. I saw this while in Prague before going to the US

[4] I feel bad to this day that I lost the ring while swimming in a pool in Cleveland; we looked for the ring on the bottom of the pool but we could not find it.

[5] My given name was Lazlo, which became the nickname Laci when we moved to Czechoslovakia. When we came to America my Aunt Bosze renamed me as Leslie, which has stuck till today. Many years later, when I applied for social security benefits, the Social Security Administration asked me for my birth certificate. I secured a birth certificate from Hungary, which spelled my last name Friedmann. I learned that when we moved to Czechoslovakia my last name was changed to Friedman.

of the gentile boys. When my father came home he knew of the incident and he said that they were blaming me. Since we were close to immigrating to America, my father decided to send me to Prague to stay with my aunt Irena to avoid further incidences from the rock throwing.

My aunt's apartment in Prague was very small, about 400 square feet but we made do. A couple from our hometown had no children and they were there, so they welcomed me to stay with them sometimes. I was there about two months. During my stay with Aunt Irena she tried to prepare me for America by teaching me how to eat properly, like holding the fork in the left hand and knife in the right hand, pushing the food unto the fork and putting the fork with the food into my mouth.[6]

Where I stayed in Prague with Aunt Irene before immigrating to the USA

When I got to America my Aunt Margaret saw me eating and told me that in America we don't eat that way. She proceeded to teach me the American way. I was happy with that, as the European method was too complicated.

[6] When I got to Aunt Margaret's home in Pennsylvania she told me, "that's not the way we eat here" and she taught me to cut my food with the knife in the right hand, then put the knife down on the plate and switch the fork to the right hand before putting the food in my mouth!

While in Prague I got to see some interesting sights, like the Charles Bridge with the statue of Jesus on a cross that had Hebrew writing across it. In the old Jewish cemetery, we saw headstones sticking out of the ground in disarray of famous Jewish sages.

In Prague, I became a baby sitter for my little cousin Edit, who was five years old. I would take her all over in her stroller. I enjoyed doing this and when I was not with her I would spend time with my cousin Ervin when he was not in school. There was a Jewish organization called *Mizrachi* and the two of us would go to meetings and dances there. One evening I met a girl there. We took a liking to each other and I remember her as my first kiss, when I was not even twelve-years old! In 1948 when we found out that in April we would be leaving for America, she and I talked about getting together in America, but she eventually wound up in Canada; given our young age, we did not stay in contact with one another.

My aunt Irena intended to leave Prague and was working on getting visas to immigrate to America, but she was having trouble because the communists were taking over Czechoslovakia. Sadly, she passed away in 1957, before she was even fifty years old. She never recovered from the death of her husband, so we could truly say she died from a broken heart. She left two children to fend for themselves. Ervin was a young adult of twenty years and he looked out for his sister, Edit who was then fourteen. After about one year they both were able to get visas to immigrate to America, sponsored by their uncle in America, Nathan Grunberger.

I was already in America with my father long before they arrived. Sadly, as much as I appreciated Aunt Irena stepping in to help provide the mothering I needed, I never saw her again once I left for America, and before she passed away.

CHAPTER 7

Immigrating to America

1947, my father and me in a passport photo

In 1938 one of my mother's sisters, Bosze, sent us papers to come to America; she offered to sponsor us. My parents acted on these papers and were assigned a quota number, but before our number came, the borders were closed and we couldn't get out anymore. This same quota number is what got us to America in 1948.

My father picked me up in Prague from aunt Irene's where I

was staying. After a long sad goodbye beginning of April 1948, we boarded a train that took us through Germany and eventually to England, crossing the English Channel to Dover, from where we took a train to London.

We spent a few days in London, seeing many of the famous sights. Then we took a train ride to Southampton, where our ship the "Queen Elizabeth" was waiting for us. It was very exciting to visit the sights that I had never seen before, but in my mind I was thinking only of America and I just wanted to just get there already. All the stories I heard from my father and the letters and packages from my aunts made me dream of a land of opportunity and I was looking forward to seeing it for myself.

The Atlantic crossing that time of the year in April was very treacherous Even for a large ship like the Queen Elizabeth that did the crossing in five days, the high seas made it very rough. Many passengers got very sick and I was one of them. I told my dad that I wanted to die. My dad was one of the ones not affected by the ship's turbulence and he tried to keep my spirits up. By the fourth day the seas had calmed and we were almost in America. When we arrived at the harbor in New York we cheered when we saw the statute of Liberty. I hold that sight in my mind and when I visit New York I make it a point to see the statute.

The Queen Elizabeth passengers were from all walks of life and only a few immigrants, as this was a few years after World War II ended. At that time, bringing valuables to America over a small denomination was against the law. My dad did manage to insert a one hundred dollar bill in the back of a toothpaste tube in such a way that the tube looked like new. My dad had lot of concern about doing this. We did not have much wealth to hide - in fact the little gold we had my dad melted down into a ring for me.

When we docked in New York my Aunt Bosze was there to greet us. Her husband was not well and was waiting for us at their apartment. We took a cab to her apartment. On the way to her apartment I couldn't stop gazing at the tall buildings. My father was wearing a suit and I was wearing a sport coat and knickers, which my dad had made for me so I would look good in America. When my aunt saw the knickers she exclaimed, "you can't wear those here?" She immediately took me to a tailor and had him turn my blousy knickers into long pants.

I was three months shy of being twelve-years old when I arrived in America on April 15 1948, which happens to coincide with the date that is very significant in the accounting profession I chose for my career, April 15 being the deadline for filing tax returns. I spoke a few words of English, but not very much. I was in for a big culture shock! We stayed with my Aunt Bosze and her husband Mike for awhile. Four of my mother's sisters who had left Europe before the war were living in the States and they came to visit.

I wound up living with my Aunt Bosze in her Manhattan apartment until summer camp started, as she made arrangements for me to go to an exclusive camp in the mountains of New York, "Camp Koko Sin" the summer after I arrived. This was quite an undertaking for me since I didn't speak English. My father went to stay with his uncle who lived in Brooklyn, which satisfied his needs, because his Uncle Shia and wife Martha kept a kosher house.

My Aunt Bosze and Uncle Mike Dorian who brought us to the USA

My aunt's instincts were right – going to this camp forced me to pick up English faster. By the end of the summer, I was able to converse with children my age in English. (It wasn't always easy. I was once involved in wrestling and I was getting instructions from the coach but we could not communicate so he sent for the headmaster who spoke some

German!) The camp was on the lake where we did a lot of canoeing; many times we would portage our canoes to nearby lakes. It was a wonderful summer and it really helped me acclimate to America. I am very grateful to my aunt for creating this opportunity for me.

That first summer after our arrival, my dad went to visit his sister Margaret in Pennsylvania while I stayed with my Aunt Bosze. Before I went to camp and after camp was over, she kept me occupied by going to many sights in New York. When my father came back from Pennsylvania they discussed the idea of me going to stay with the sister he had just visited. His reasoning was that my Aunt Bosze in New York had given up many of the Orthodox ways from which she came from and my father was still in that mode; his sister in Pennsylvania was still Sabbath observant. (Many years later I found out that my Aunt Bosze wanted to adopt me, since she and her husband had no children. My dad would not go that route.)

Brother Marv and family, my parents, Uncle Sol and Aunt Margaret

My dad's sister Margaret and her husband Sol with their son Herbie lived in a small town in Pennsylvania that had only a few Jewish families living there. They were living there because they owned a dress store in town. They were very religious and uncle Sol would go daily to the nearby city Pottsville, five miles away, for morning *minyan*. Occasionally when he did not go to the morning service he would put on his *tefillin* and pray at home. My father was committed to keeping the Sabbath and he could not get a job without working Saturdays anywhere except in New York so he chose for me to live in Pennsylvania with his sister, Margaret, while he stayed in New York to look for work.

*1950 Brooklyn,
me and my father*

*Aunt Mancy, her husband Paul Fonda,
and cousin Peter. I stayed with them
summer of '51 in Waukegen, Il*

*1950 Brooklyn, my father, my father's Uncle Shmuel
and his wife Martha, their daughter-in law, her child, and me*

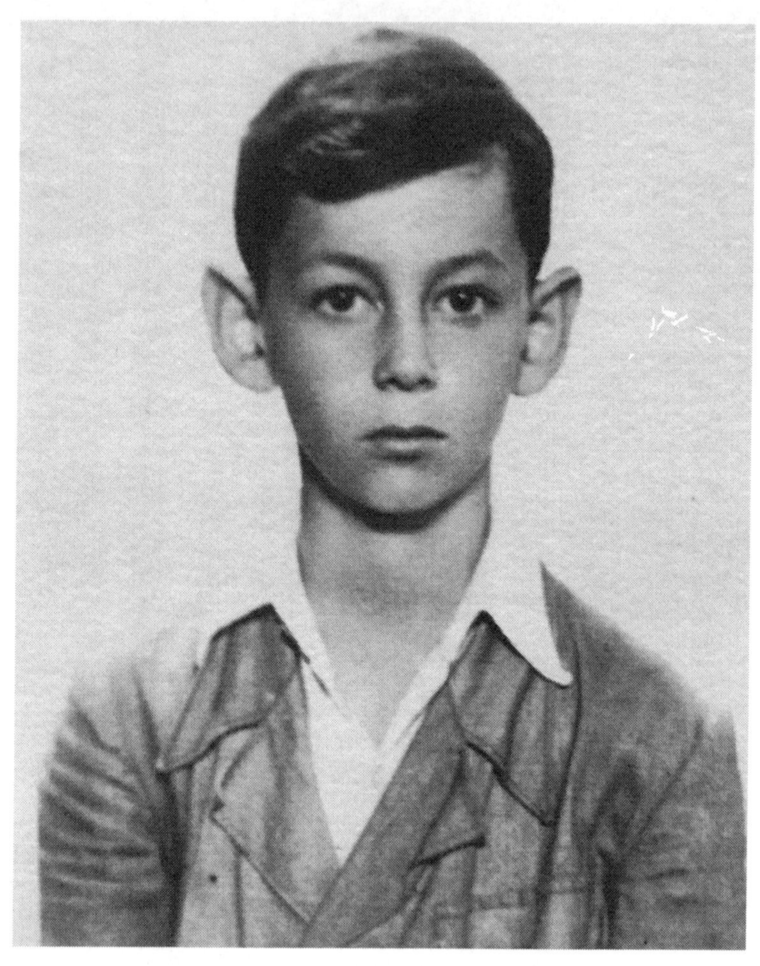

1953 citizenship photo

CHAPTER 8

My High School Years in America

After my first summer in New York, I moved to be with my Aunt Margaret and Uncle Sol, in Pennsylvania and I started school in September. Unbelievably, because I could still barely speak or understand English, (despite my fast-track English classes in summer camp) they enrolled me in the first grade, even though I was twelve years old! Thankfully, as I quickly learned the language, they kept moving me up to the next grade, so by the time the year was up, I was in the 5th grade. Then throughout all of my future schooling, I remained one year behind classmates of my age.

While going to school in *Schuylkill Haven* and skipping grades, I never learned to spell words properly. I would use my Slovak pronunciation phonetically to memorize words. I have had this problem all my life and always struggled with some words. Speaking languages was quite different. I learned quickly how to speak in English without an accent, with help from my Uncle Sol, who taught me where to place my teeth and tongue to say the words correctly.[1]

While I was living with my Aunt Margaret and Uncle Sol, every day one of them would give me money to buy a milk shake, since I was so thin. It did not help. I was very strong and it did not bother me to be thin, even though it seemed to bother the adult caretakers in my life. I stayed thin until I was in my fifties!

To her credit, my Aunt Bosze still treated me like her own son and did many things for me throughout my teenage years in America. Whenever I would come to New York to visit, she took me to many attractions such as Rockefeller Plaza where we watched ice-skating and ate ice cream from silver goblets. I could always count on her for my monthly twenty dollar check, which she continued for years, until I got married.

My cousin Herbie was graduating from high school and their married daughter Trudy and husband Bob who was a dentist, along with their two children, were already living in Cleveland, so my aunt and uncle decided to move to Cleveland to be closer to family, and to make it easier for Herbie to find a job. The decision was made that I would move with them to Cleveland.

Before leaving *Schuylkill Haven* a large package of clothing arrived from cousins in Detroit. My aunt put out the word that I could use clothing and they responded, only my cousin was much heavier than me and the beautiful leather coat included was much too big for me. It was not all wasted, as some things my aunt had altered to fit me.

[1] Interestingly I was born in Hungary and exposed to Hungarian but I did not speak it well as I went to Slovak school and the government was trying to instill in Slovakia that everyone should be Slovak and we were almost forbidden to speak another language. Therefore in the house we tried to communicate in Slovak even though my parents would find Hungarian to be easier. When I came to the United States at first I spoke Hungarian with all my relatives since they did not speak Slovak. I was brushing up on my on Hungarian in the meantime and over time I forgot how to speak Slovak fluently other than words here and there. Even my Hungarian has gotten weak since I don't have whom to speak with. I did find this past year a Holocaust survivor in our community who speaks fluent Hungarian and I've been practicing with him my Hungarian!

In 1949 when school let out we left for Cleveland. Herbie went by train ahead of us. I sat in the backseat of my aunt and uncle's 1937 Pontiac. Luckily, even though the car was twelve years old, we made the long trek without incident.

When we arrived in Cleveland, Trudy had rented for us the upstairs of a two family home only a couple of blocks from her home. I shared a bedroom with Herbie, which was fine with me. I liked him even though we didn't have much in common since he was five years older than me.

My aunt made arrangements for me to go to the Hebrew Academy, a Jewish day school in Cleveland, which turned out not to my liking since the hours were very long. A station wagon would pick me up at 6:30 am and I wouldn't return home until 6 pm. Between these long hours and the curriculum that consisted of entire morning of learning Hebrew and the afternoon English classes, along with being the last off the bus, and almost being too late for dinner, it wasn't a very workable situation for me. I will say though, the school was wonderful with very good teachers and I learned a lot there.[2]

The kids were all very nice and I got along with them and played sports with them during recess. Unfortunately where they lived, and I lived was too far apart to play any time except during school. Even though I lived far from my school friends, I lived across the street from an elementary school and made many friends there. We played sports and hung out at the playground.

From the time I came to Cleveland my cousin Trudy was my mentor, helping me with my schoolwork, buying me clothes and giving me advice. In return, I would babysit for their two

[2] While attending Hebrew Academy, they provided lunch, which was either peanut butter and jelly sandwich or cream cheese and jelly sandwich. I always chose the cream cheese and jelly, since I never even heard of peanut butter. I know this is hard to believe but till this day, I've never eaten a peanut butter sandwich. The European snack was an open slice of bread with some kind of spread on it, not two slices of bread with something in between. I recollect my mother and I sitting in the kitchen or on the porch eating such a snack. It is a precious memory I have of my mother.

children. She insisted on paying me even though I felt I was more than compensated with her generosity. When Trudy and Bob were planning a late evening I would sleep over at their house. I was a very capable babysitter since I had gained experience from taking care of my little cousin in Czechoslovakia.

I did have one situation while babysitting at my cousin's house. One early evening after the kids went to bed I went down to the basement and found an air rifle. I set up a target and practiced hitting the target. After a while, I got pretty good at it. One day I took the air rifle outside and decided to use the street parking sign as my target. The next day the neighbor across the street contacted my cousin about the holes in their front window! Apparently when I was shooting at the parking sign, I must've missed a few times and hit their window! Trudy replaced the windows and I paid her back with my babysitting money. All's well that ends well. A few years later, I accidentally put an electric plug into my mouth, which caused a horrific injury, which I'll tell you about later. The window I broke belonged to the doctor who took care of me when I was hospitalized. Small world indeed.

Soon after that incident, Trudy and her family moved to Los Angeles, California because her husband was drafted into the Navy. I certainly missed all of them.

The summer of 1949, I celebrated my bar mitzvah. I took lessons from a private tutor after we came to Cleveland in June and did my presentation in a small temple a month later. My father came in from New York where he was living and working. My aunt made me a nice party and all our relatives came. We had many cousins living in Cleveland. Right after my party I went to Brooklyn with my dad, and from there I went to summer camp.

The family got me a bicycle for my bar mitzvah, which I wanted very much. It reminded me of getting the pedal car I so wanted when I was four years old. I drove the bike around and pretended that I was driving my pedal car around the gas station in Micahalovce. I tried to convince my aunt that I should go to public school the following school year, but she wouldn't go for it, so I went back to the Hebrew

July 1949. My Bar Mitzvah

Academy and completed my seventh grade there.

In the summers of 1949 and 1950, I was in my father's care in Brooklyn, although a good bit of my summers were taken up with summer camp. Dad had an apartment there and went to work on weekdays and Sunday. We would take the subway and go to Far Rockaway Beach or to Coney Island; we had a good time and these are very happy memories for me. When I wasn't away at summer camp, during the days while he was working, I would keep busy playing stickball or handball in the street where the apartment was. Also on Saturday we would go to temples where famous cantors sang. Some Saturdays we would go to one or two temples and listen to the renditions of cantors. I have records from some of these famous cantors and still enjoy listening to this music.

The first summer my dad made arrangements for me to attend a religious Jewish camp for part of the summer, where the expectation of the boys was to spend most of the time studying. I was very unhappy about this, and I asked him in our weekly phone conversation to please bring me home. That did not happen since I was there because my father's temple was doing him a favor in exchange for leading the services at the temple and they made arrangements for me to attend at no cost. I stuck it out and at least enjoyed playing some soccer when we had free time in the afternoon. This camp was so unlike the camp my aunt sent me to the previous year, which was only for fun, not learning, It was a really difficult adjustment for me, and left such a bitter taste that I never went to camp again. The summer of 1950, I stuck it out in Brooklyn for the whole summer without going away to camp.

Seventh grade Hebrew Academy. I am bottom right wearing sportcoat

I returned to Cleveland after the summer of 1950, to continue school in the yeshiva there. I was living with my aunt on Kinsman, which I did from the day I arrived in Cleveland until I finished the 7th grade. I played a lot of softball across the street from our house at Rickoff elementary school. One day a kid who was not playing with us started making fun of us and I took objection to it. We started pushing each other and even though he was bigger than me by some fifty pounds, we wrestled on cinder-covered ground until we were both exhausted. We were bloody and I returned to my house and went to the basement to clean at least the visible areas of blood so that my aunt did not see that I was involved in a fight.

During the school year my father visited me in Cleveland. During that year, while visiting me, he was introduced to Cecilia

Green, originally from Hungary, who was living in Cleveland with cousins.

Cecilia spent the war years in the concentration camp, Bergen Belsen. She was taken out on a stretcher to Sweden where she spent months recuperating from malnutrition and typhus. The rest of her life she would endure the effects of her time in the concentration camp. She spoke Hungarian, and so did I, which made our communication easy. In fact, she had trouble learning English, and I was helpful to her in learning how to speak English. She was eight years younger than my father, and a very hard worker who worked full time in the sweater factory.[3]

My dad made several trips to Cleveland, and it became clear to me that my father had found a woman he intended to marry. I was happy for him, but I felt ambivalent about it, especially because I did not know her at all. The summer of 1951 Aunt Mancy, one of my mother's sisters who lived in Rockford Illinois with her husband Paul and their four year old son Peter, invited me go there for part of the summer. While I was there playing ball with Peter I fell backwards and hurt my left arm. I never told anyone and hid it from every one for the few weeks that I was there. After a couple of months, the injury healed, but I found out later in life that it had been a rotator cuff injury, which would give me some trouble in my later years.

On June 5, 1951, my father married Cecilia in a simple ceremony in the rabbi's study in Cleveland. They were married several months before I could call her by a name. She finally sat down with me and we resolved that I would call her "Cili." She understood that at age fifteen I would have a hard time calling her mother. After they were married they started a household in Cleveland and I finally, after many years, got to live with my father every day and not just in the summer. My dad made a big decision in that in order to move to Cleveland he had to give up the idea of not working on Sabbath as he could only find work that entailed working on the Sabbath. I think

[3] When we were in public and my parents would speak Hungarian I would be very embarrassed and ask that they stop.

this meant a lot to him but he felt he had no choice.

My aunt and uncle, decided to move out to Los Angeles to be closer to Trudy and her family. My aunt and uncle moving worked out well since it was very hard to find homes to rent and we were able to move into the house my aunt was renting. With my aunt gone, I was off the hook from attending the religious school I didn't really want to attend anymore.

And so in September of 1951, I started 8th grade at Alexander Hamilton Jr. High School. I was very happy there and made many friends. It was a very long walk to school but walking in groups made it go faster. There also was a streetcar we could take, but it was costly unless you bought a weekly pass, which most of us couldn't afford.

While going to school at Alexander Hamilton, I had a teacher who claimed to able to tell by a person's accent where they came from. She demonstrated that skill and she was right - when it was my turn to speak, she said I come from Pennsylvania. I told her that's where I learned to speak but I come from Hungary. After I explained my whereabouts she understood.

As soon as I turned age fourteen I got a working permit from the school. I worked in a grocery store where I did odd jobs. In the evenings I would go to the Hillel house for music, dancing and camaraderie. It was here that I met my best friend Howard Ehrlich (who also was instrumental in introducing me to my wife, that story to be shared later). We had school classes together and it was in typesetting class that I would tell him about my war experiences. In the past I had not shared my Holocaust trauma with anyone. Howard has always remained my best friend; even when I moved to another school we were constantly in contact. After Howard finished school he eventually moved to Los Angeles and opened several delis and retired in Los Angeles. I'm sure he'll get a kick out of reading this memoir. Howard, his wife Joan and children are all living in LA. We have from time to time visited each other either in Florida or in LA.

While I was working at the grocery store, Howard was working in a nearby delicatessen and was instrumental in my going to work at

Les, Barbara and Howard, our matchmaker, high school graduation

Sam and Jerry's Deli. There, I learned how to cut lox and corned beef and the art of making a good sandwich. These skills came in handy, enabling me to earn money all throughout college. To this day my kids request and I still enjoy making trays for our family holidays and gatherings.

I was living with my parents on Kinsman, attending 9th grade at Alexander Hamilton Jr. High and one evening a friend, Marvin, (whom I had met at Hillel) and I took a bike ride to Cleveland Heights, about a 45-minute ride. Once we got there we stopped at a pharmacy on the corner of Cedar and Taylor. While we were having a soda in the pharmacy some kids took apart our bikes and when we came outside the kids outside were laughing at us and one of the boys punched my friend in the face. I felt really bad for my friend since he had a heart condition and I was very concerned about him. We took our bikes and parts down the street and managed to somehow assemble them and ride home.

I hadn't had an incident like this since I was a kid in Europe; I suspected at the time that it was an anti-Semitic act, but I never found out who these kids were. I believe they were part of a gang.

Thankfully, it turned out that my friend was okay other than having a bloody nose.

I attended John Adams High School for half a year when my parents moved to another neighborhood that was in the Glenville area; I had to transfer to Glenville High School after we moved into a new rental home. I needed to quit my job at Sam and Jerry's when we moved to Glenville.

Right before starting my new school in Glenville, I incurred a serious accident that almost cost my life. My father and I were measuring a headboard to fit on the wall and I picked up an electrical cord that was lying on the ground. I did not realize that it was a hot plug so I put it in my mouth so it would not fall from my hand. I burned my tongue very badly; the doctor I went to see (the one whose window I broke), demonstrated what electricity could do by putting a screwdriver in the electrical socket and I watched as the screw driver melted at the end!

This was an incredibly painful injury initially and for several days thereafter. The electric plug that wound up in my mouth burned a hole in my tongue this caused the tongue to swell and I had to drink only liquids until my tongue healed. Anyway, injury withstanding, it was time to start my new school and I was not able to speak. Worse than that, I had to hold a hanky to my mouth so that I would not drool! As you can imagine, it was very difficult for me to make friends in the new school for the first month. But then, I eventually got friendly with the kids that I walked to school with. Since it was almost a two-mile walk, that gave us plenty of time to talk – once I could talk!

I made a close friend with Allan Micenmacher, who lived on the next street over from me. He too was a Holocaust survivor, coming from Poland. I met him on the playground playing soccer. He went to a different high school than me, but we played all kinds of sports together, and as close as Howard was to me, so was Allan. I was close friends with Allan for many years, and even did his taxes for him until he retired. We didn't see each other, even though he was living in Cleveland. Several years ago he moved to Arizona. Maybe when this memoir is finished I'll locate him and give him a copy for his enjoyment!

Glenville had some wonderful teachers and I got to know my gym teacher very well. He encouraged me to go out for sports since I impressed him in gym with my ability. In gym class they put up a pole for us to try high jumping and I had no problem clearing six feet, which amazed the coach since I was only about 5 ft. 6 inches and weighed less than 100 pounds. I was built for cross country running and Mr. Civileto, our coach, wanted me to go out for the track team. I told him that I couldn't do it since I had a job after school in the deli from 3 pm until dinnertime, with Monday off since the store was closed, and I worked four to eight hours a day on Saturdays and Sundays.

As soon as I was better from my accident, Jerry from Sam & Jerry Delicatessen called me and asked if I could return to working for him on weekends as he needed help. He was willing to pick me up and bring me home, since this was at least a five-mile ride each way. I did this for a while but then it became too much of a hassle and Jerry was able to get a new employee.

Then, I was able to get a job at Alberts Deli right in my neighborhood. So this would be my third deli job – you could say I was becoming a true expert in the world of deli! This job I enjoyed, and the owners, Albert and Libby Feuerwerker treated me as if I was their son. They were both Holocaust survivors and they did not have any other children. I worked behind the deli counter, stocked shelves and did for them one of the more disliked jobs - reaching into a big herring barrel and pulling out a fish and wrapping it in paper.

I continued working at Alberts because I enjoyed working there. On Sunday customers were lined up to get their quarter pound of lox, and I took pleasure that I could cut and flip the lox into piece of wax paper and most of the time when I would put it on the scale it would be exactly a quarter of a pound! The atmosphere was interesting to me – many of the customers were Holocaust survivors, and they spoke Yiddish, which helped me learn how to converse in Yiddish as well. The Jewishness certainly was awakened in me, as many of the customers were from eastern part of Europe near where I once lived. The area was called Marmarosh and these customers were mostly very religious, yet most of them had to give up being shomer shabbos to live and work in this part of America. Most of these Jews became successful businessmen in the real estate trades, homebuilders, carpenters, electricians, bricklayers, etc.[4]

As part of my job, I would go on deliveries with Albert, especially during Passover. It was here that I learned to drive, as he would let me drive on many occasions. The store was located about half way from my house and the school, which made it very convenient for walking from school and than home after work. When I got home I would have to change clothes and wash up, as the fishy smell from the store was very strong.

I continued working at Alberts until I graduated from high school, on weekends when I was in college, and full time over the summers. It was a formative experience of my youth. Both of my parents worked very hard to pay the rent and bills. My father was a salesman of notions, working on commission. He worked hard to improve his English, and as he did, his orders increased, and so did his pay. My parents did not want any money from me and encouraged me to save my working money for college, which I did.

It turned out that Cili was as good to me as a real mom could be. Besides working all day long, she also did all the cooking and cleaning at home, and then as a side business, she made draperies for customers from our house. My father would go to the homes, take measurements and install the drapes she made.

Two years after my parents were married, on June 12, 1953, my family experienced a true miracle. My much-younger brother, Marvin, was born to my father and stepmother, even though doctors had told my stepmother that her Holocaust trauma had made it

[4] After I started practicing accounting on my own some of these customers became my clients.

impossible for her ever to have children. I was able to enjoy family again, with a baby brother who was only two years old when I graduated high school and went off to OSU.

High school reunion class of 1955

My in-laws, Julius & Helen Gelfand

CHAPTER 9

Meeting Barbara & Going to College

While a senior in high school, I met my wife Barbara through a double date set up with my friend Howard. As fate would have it, Barbara was actually Howard's date, and he set me up with her friend. But Barbara and I hit it off immediately. She invited me to a BBG party, but only after she cleared it with Howard. From this date on Barb and I had an exclusive relationship. Barb was going to be 16 and I was going to be 18. We fell in love with each other, a love that has lasted till this day. The expression "childhood sweethearts" applies!

I started dating Barbara and we would be going back-and-forth between the Heights area where she lives and she would come down to see me at work in the city. I was invited to her sweet 16 birthday dinner with her parents and conservative that I am, I bought her a hair dryer. (Years later she told me that a portable hair dryer was not a romantic present, but what did I know? I hadn't seriously dated a girl before!)

Whenever I wasn't in school or working I would be with her. Her parents liked me so I would join her family at a very nice restaurant for dinner most Sunday evenings. (Later I would comment that my parents did not spend in a whole week as much as one Sunday evening when I joined Barbara's family for dinner!)

The food I ate at home was traditional Jewish Hungarian food. Friday night we enjoyed traditional chicken soup with boiled chicken, potato and vegetables. The leftover chicken would be repurposed into several other meals during the week. I was so accustomed to this ethnic food, I'd never even eaten a slice of pizza until I started dating Barb and she introduced it to me. I liked it, as well as several other American foods I enjoyed after being exposed to them.

While I was dating Barb, I purchased a new 1953 Chevy. My father had to sign the papers since I was under age; however I paid the down payment on the car and promised to make the monthly payments. At that point my father did not have a driver's license so after we got the new car I actually taught him to drive and then he got his license!

This driving almost every night to Barb's house was objectionable to my father and he started commenting that I was too hard on the car. We had a disagreement and I gave him the car with the payment book. Cili, my stepmother, spoke to her friend in the used car business about getting me another car. I wound up purchasing a 1948 Hudson Hornet for $200! This car was huge- like my friends would joke, I could put the whole football team in this car. It drove ok but you get what you pay for sometimes – it always needed maintenance and after about a year I had to scrap the car, as it was too expensive to fix. Then I wound up using my dad's car – the one that used to be mine.

This time he didn't give me a hard time – he saw that the used car I bought cost me a lot of money and he was sorry he took the other car away from me. About the same time Barb's father bought her a car, so we always had transportation.

For my 18th birthday Barb threw me a surprise party at her house. I was in shock and even cried since I never had a birthday party before, except for my bar mitzvah. My childhood was anything but normal and birthday parties were not part of it at all.

The year 1954 was a big year for me. I was 18-years old and the future was bright. I was very happy to be dating Barbara. When I graduated high school I didn't expect to go to college. I was committed to Barbara, and I planned to keep working in the deli and maybe own my own deli someday. But both Barbara and my stepmother encouraged me to go to college. Cili would point out how successful my cousin Bob was in becoming a dentist and she thought I should do the same. I had been saving my money from working and had enough for two years of college.

With my family and Barbara's blessing, I enrolled in Ohio State University in the fall of 1955 with dentistry being my preference. I planned to complete two years of pre-dentistry and then try to get into dental school on a working program that would pay for my schooling and board, since my parents could not financially support me.

When I graduated high school in the summer of 1955 I celebrated with both my family and Barb's. My Aunt Bosze sent me a gold watch with an inscription on the back that read, "Congratulations Leslie, Mike and Bosze." I wore this watch for over 40 years and I still have it as a keepsake.

Who could have imagined when I was just a boy of seven in the midst of war that I would someday be living in the land of opportunity and headed to college? Life started out rough for me but it was turning out really well.

I left Barbara and my family and traveled to Ohio State University in Columbus, Ohio, about a two-hour drive away. Howard and I roomed together in a rooming house just off campus. We decided to rush a couple of fraternities and after awhile we went in separate directions: Howard decided he was not going to join a fraternity and I wound up joining PHI EP, because a lot of the guys were Clevelanders, and it was a small friendly group. I began eating my meals at the fraternity house, and Howard and I didn't see each other as much.

In fact, after a year, Howard became very disillusioned with college and college life and decided to quit school and return to Cleveland. (He prospered in the deli business and opened up several restaurants in California, so not having a college degree had no negative impact on him. Howard knew what he wanted and he was very good at it and turned out to be a successful businessman).

Meanwhile, after the first quarter at OSU, I had to move into the fraternity house since that was a requirement that you spend at least one quarter in the house, in addition to the quarter while pledging. There I made friends with Bob Turoff, Mert Walters, Denny Harris and Mike Appel. I went through a humbling and harrowing hell week experience with Mert and Mike, which I will never forget, and I'm actually glad I experienced. (And it must remain secret!) Bob, Mert and Denny were to become my roommates when we moved out of the frat house.[1]

During my first year at OSU I discovered that my cousin Herbie was also enrolled there as a freshman. He had served in the army two years and got married to Judy from Columbus, Ohio and had a two-year-old son Steve. We did some studying together for the finals.[2]

I was studying hard, or so I thought, and I joined the soccer team. At that time a freshman could not play on the varsity team - they had to play on the JV, Junior Varsity. Since I played soccer most of my life I was a much better player than most of the players, with the exception of a couple of boys from Latin America. This was the first time since I started working that I was free to play sports and I loved it. I played soccer every afternoon at the school. The practices lasted till after the meals that were being served at the fraternity house and my friends at the house kept the meals warm for me.

[1] Mert died a few years ago but we still see Carol, his widow. Bob's wife passed away but we see him with Maxine his significant other often. Denny is a doctor in Phoenix, and we catch up with each other occasionally in our travels.

[2] After I left OSU Herbie and family moved to California to be with the rest of his family. Herbie and Judy had two more children, Marla and Debra.

The highlight of my soccer career happened near the end of the season when the JV's scrimmage against the Varsity resulted in a tie score between the two teams.

That was a great first year for me, but reality set in. Just like in years past, my focus had to shift to making enough money to pay for my schooling, and I no longer had the liberty to take so much time for just plain fun. So soccer became a first-year sport only. The fact that Barbara was also going to be attending OSU my second year was another consideration in my giving up soccer, so I could spend more time with her.

My time needed to be focused on my highest priorities – staying connected to Barbara, which involved visits back home and her coming to visit me, my studies, and making the money I needed to finish my degree. During my freshman year whenever I could get home to see Barbara, I would. I'd also put in some time working at Alberts, so my deli years continued. I would either take a train or hitch hike wearing my ROTC uniform, which made it very easy to get a ride.

I can honestly say that cold cuts and lox paid for my college degree! I made a practical decision during my first year of college, to go into accounting rather then pursue a dental career, once I realized how long the process was to become a dentist and how much money I'd have to come up with. That decision ultimately served me very well.

Before completing the first year of school, my three buddies and me left the frat house and rented two apartments in a building - one would be for Bob and me and the other for Denny and Mert. Since the apartments were off-campus and we needed transportation to go to school, Denny and Mert had cars and we made a pledge to one another that all four of us would use the two cars as necessary. The apartment Bob and I shared was called an efficiency – we shared one large bedroom with a bathroom and kitchen off this room.

So my first year in college was working out great. My studies were going well, I was enjoying my fraternity friendships, and my off-campus housing was sufficient for my needs. Barbara and I were managing to keep our long-distance relationship as strong as it had ever been. Life was good.

You might wonder where my family was during this time, since my entire world seemed to be college and Barbara. My parents participated in my school activities such as parents weekend and I lived with them until I got married – more about that in the next chapter.

Barbara and her younger sister Marlene with her parents

Barbara and her parents Julius and Helen Gelfand

Barbara and Marlene,
with mother and grandmother

Fraternity brother and roommate
Dr. Denny Harris and me

Bob Turoff was my
roommate at OSU

Mike, Mert and I went through Hell Week together.
Mike, Mert, Les and Denny

Denny, Bob, Mert and me

CHAPTER 10

Engaged and Married!

I mentioned that I shared a room with Bob. I also shared that Barbara told me many years later that my gift to her on her sweet sixteenth birthday was not the most romantic of choices. Well the pattern continued: In June of 1955, when I graduated from high school, that summer Barb and I spent all our time together and it was then that I knew that she was the one I wanted to spend the rest of my life with.

The second year at OSU I shared a one-room apartment with my roommate, Bob. He was sleeping in his bed, and Barbara was sitting on my bed when I got down on one knee and proposed to her! Thank God she accepted, and on April 19 1957, Barbara made me the happiest man in the world when she said yes.

We wanted to marry the coming September in 1957. We had to convince both of our parents that we could do this. Now that I was second year of accounting studies, I prepared a cash flow budget that I was very proud of and presented it to my father-in-law. He wouldn't even look at it. Instead he just said, "Well if you guys want

Barb and Les, 9-15-1957

to get married, what can I do about it?" Both of Barbara's parents liked me and were happy about our engagement. My parents were also very happy about it. The date was set for September 15, 1957 to get married, which meant that I still had two years of college left.

I pause for a moment in my storytelling to reflect on how important Barb's parents and family came to be for me.

I had a very close relationship with Barb's parents, Julius and Helen Gelfand, and Barb's younger sister Marlene who was four years younger than Barb. Unfortunately my mother-in-law died in 1970 at the young age of fifty-seven from ovarian cancer. Barbara and I had been in California when she became severely ill; we returned to Cleveland and managed to get to the hospital the day before she passed away. Our son Lee was twelve years old at that time, Douglas was nine and Lisa was seven so she knew our children and she was a wonderful grandmother to them. The kids loved her. After she died, my father in law showed little interest in remarrying for a long time. He would come to our home every evening to have dinner with our family, watch the news with me, play with the kids and then go back to his apartment.

Some time later, Julius started to go out with a long time family friend, Bess, whose husband had died many years before. Julius and Bess were on vacation in Las Vegas when Bess had a heart attack and died. After that tragedy, he was introduced to Rose, and married her shortly thereafter. He was with Rose for many years, before Julius passed in 1989. Rose lived until 1996, spending several years in a nursing home. After she died, as executor and trustee of her estate, I helped her daughter Arlene who was designated as the beneficiary of most of the estate with a minor portion going to her stepdaughters, Barbara and Marlene. Rose made clear in her will that she wanted to make sure that Arlene would have funds to sustain herself for many years, since she was divorced and had only her income from being a nurse. I invested the money and sent Arlene a monthly check until I was permitted by the will's instructions to distribute the remaining funds to Arlene and to close the trust.

I will never forget the kindness shown to me when I first met Barb and her parents. They were a wonderful addition to the family that I already had. I know there was a special bond between Julius and myself, as he also came to the United States as a twelve-year-old child from Russia, and shared a lot of experiences adjusting to life in the United States.

Helen tried to please me as well, for example, when she made gefilte fish, first serving it warm and then cold, to serve it to me the way I liked it. (The first time I was served the warm fish, I was not expecting that and showed an immediate dislike, although, I did not mean to.) After that she tried so hard to please me in anything she did. I loved them for their kindness to Barb, our children and myself.

I also want to acknowledge the lavish holiday celebrations and delicious food that my mother-in-law prepared for all of us to enjoy and for our children to know the meaning of the celebrations. They were just the best in-laws and grandparents to our children that I could ever ask for.

Now, back to my story – and before Barb and I married:

When Barb started her freshman year at OSU in September 1956, she had no idea that before she would finish her freshman year her plans would change. Our plans were for Barb to quit school at the end of that year and I would transfer to Kent State University and commute since I was able to get to my job at Alberts Deli and Barb got a job working for an escrow company.

Before we got married we rented an apartment that we liked and which would be ready for us to occupy when we return from our honeymoon. It was located where Barb could take a bus to work and I would take the car on my commute to Kent State, which was about twenty miles from the apartment. I commuted with four or five other commuters with similar schedules. We would leave school around noon, which worked out fine for me, so I could work in Mr. Kaplan's accounting office in the afternoon.

Before we were married I got a notice from Kent State that I would have to be present for orientation since I was a transfer student.

This meant our planned honeymoon to Florida would be cut short and it made it impractical to go there. Therefore we decided to drive to Niagara Falls for our honeymoon.

Our wedding plans included getting married at my father's temple since he wanted an Orthodox wedding rather then a Reform one that my future in-laws belonged to. My future in-laws understood, since their roots at one time had been Orthodox and then changed to Reform. Part of the preliminary schedule included meeting with the Rabbi Engelberg from my father's synagogue, Taylor Road Synagogue, who met with both of us and conversed about each of our backgrounds in Judaism. I told the rabbi that I attended the Hebrew Academy of Cleveland and was bar mitzvah and studied *Gemara*. The Rabbi was impressed. Then he proceeded to ask Barb what her background was and she told him that she went through Silvers Temple and was confirmed from there. And the Rabbi responded, "You put in time." Barb was very upset upon hearing this and afterwards told me that Rabbi Abba Hillel Silver of Silvers Temple knew her by her first name and he was willing to do a dual ceremony, but the Rabbi from the Taylor Road synagogue would not have it.

I felt bad, since I regarded Rabbi Silver as almost a God-like figure after going to many of his lectures and sermons with my future father-in-law. When I thought of his accomplishments- that in 1948 he spoke for Israel at the United Nations and helped Israel become an independent nation - that impressed me even more.

At first I had had a problem with not wearing a yarmulke; although it wasn't mandatory I felt out of place if I wore one.

My wife's family respected my family's wishes to have an Orthodox wedding and therefore they did not interfere and the Orthodox Rabbi from the temple married us. He initially asked Barb to go to the mikveh before we got married, but she told me that was a deal breaker for her, so we exchanged vows without this ritual.

The wedding was wonderful. It turned out to be a huge wedding as my father-in-law knew many people and sent out invitations accordingly. He also put no limitations on my parents as to how many invitations they could send out. We had approximately 500 people at the wedding celebrating with us. The music, dancing and food could not have been any better. My aunts on my mother's side came in from out of town. I was most happy that my Aunt Bosze was there. (Although after seeing such a big wedding, she stopped sending her regular checks because she figured my in-laws must have been helping us! Little did she know how much we could use her help.)

Our wedding, 9-15-57.
L are my parents, R are Barb's parents

The wedding ceremony was beautiful. Howard was best man and my fraternity brothers Bob, Denny, Mert and Mike were the ushers. Barb's maid of honor was her sister Marlene and bridesmaids were Ilene, Sandy, and Annette.

Barbara's father had given us the convertible that Barbara was driving for a wedding present. It was a peach and white 1955 Plymouth. Over the summer I helped keep the car clean; since it had a white top it would to get dirty and I would scrub it with a brush to get it clean.

When we got to Niagara Falls we followed the tour buses and saw all the sights. We were there for just one week because I had to be back at Kent State by September 27 for orientation.

On our way back to Cleveland we noticed that there was some air coming in from the front of the car and the next thing we knew, the canvas top flew off and was trailing behind the car. It was getting cold and it seemed like we were just dodging rain. We made it back to Cleveland but I wound up with a very bad head cold. When Barb called my parents and told them that I was not feeling well they offered some remedies. Barb wanted to take me to the doctor the next day but they said to her that it was the High Holidays and she shouldn't drive me to see the doctor. The next day Barb drove me to the doctor and he prescribed some cough syrup and medication and told me to go home and rest, and thankfully I was fine in a few days.

Getting started on our honeymoon

We settled into our new apartment and a happy married life with one another, one that thankfully continues for both of us till this day!

When my brother Marvin was seven years old, in 1960, soon after my graduation from Kent State University, my parents decided to move to California. My Aunt Margaret, my father's sister now lived in California and she was very instrumental in having my parents and brother move out there. My stepmother's concentration camp ordeal left her frail and very susceptible to illness in the cold weather. Therefore they decided that it would be best for them to move out there. I was sorry to see them go, as they were my only immediate family left in Cleveland besides some distant cousins.

We did get to see each other annually, as they would come here to Cleveland and I would go to California to see them. I am fortunate that I was now happily married to Barbara and very close to her family, so that took some of the sting out of being so far away from my own family.

Lee, Lisa, and Doug

Lee, Doug, and Lisa

CHAPTER 11

The Birth of Our Children

When we returned from our honeymoon we already had our apartment fixed up. We were ready and excited about the next phase of our lives. I started commuting to Kent State University with a group of guys and we alternated driving. My classes started at 8 am and ended by noon each day. My father-in-law secured me a part-time job with Mr. Kaplan in an accounting office for the afternoons.

Meanwhile, Barb took a bus to a job downtown. On the weekends, I kept up my job at Alberts Deli. Then the owner of the accounting office Mr. Kaplan asked me if I would go to one of his clients, Mr. Cyncynatus, on Thursday evenings, to make out their payroll and pay their bills. Every other evening, I was focused on my studies. This job ended up lasting many years and after I graduated college I did their personal accounting as well. Paul Cyncynatus was a painting contractor and he and his wife were Holocaust survivors from Poland, as well as their nephew Henrik who worked in the business with them. Paul's wife Ann did the office work and Henrik was a superintendent on jobs. Henrik was in the army as a master sergeant, a status he retained by joining the National Guard. After Paul died Henrik took over running their business. Mr. Kaplan did not know that I was a Holocaust survivor when he asked me to work for the Cyncynatus family. I'm very glad he put us together.

Our son Lee was born

There's a famous saying: Man plans and God laughs. Our plan for Barbara to work while I finished school was a decent plan, but she became pregnant with our son Lee who was born on August 6, 1958, less than 11 months after we married. Barbara was a trooper and worked all through the pregnancy, but we made plans after the baby was born to give up the apartment and move in with my in-laws. We took over Barb's old bedroom and we put a crib in it and managed very nicely, with my in-law's help, for the next 8 months. Barb still had a younger sister living at home, which presented no problem as we all got along very nicely. Barbara's parents treated me as a son and I in turn respected and idolized them.

Lee's bar mitzvah

It bothered me a lot to feel like a burden to my in-laws, so I continued working my three part-time jobs in order to help make our expenses. It's a good thing Barbara had a lot of family around, because I was always busy. I have to wonder how I did it. Besides being a new husband, taking courses at Kent State, and working three jobs, I was now a new father of a son, and I was all of 22-years old!

When I saw that we could financially make rent in an apartment, we moved out of my in-laws house and into a new two-bedroom apartment in Mayfield Heights. It was a new garden style one-story building with a swimming pool and a courtyard; we made many friends there.

My in-laws continued to help us anyway they could. We would regularly go to their house for Friday night dinner and my mother-in-law would raid the freezer and cupboard and make care packages that would last for several days.

In the fall of 1960, I was a proud graduate with an accounting degree from Kent State University. At my graduation, my son was one and my brother was seven. It was shortly after my graduation that my parents and Marvin moved to California. I was particularly fortunate to be so connected to my in-laws when my family moved so far away.

After my graduation I went to work full time for Mr. Kaplan for whom I had been working part time in his accounting office. He made me a fair offer and jobs were very hard to get.

Barb was a stay at home mom taking care of Lee and the household, which was customary in those days. Soon I put Barb to work typing tax returns that I hand wrote. There were no fax machines, copy machines, or computers in those days. In fact the typing of the tax returns was difficult since we had to make three copies using carbon paper!

Our son Doug was born

Our second son Doug was born on August 25, 1961. I was working at Cyncynatus when I got a call from Barb to take her to hospital. Doug was born that morning.

In those days fathers did not go into birthing rooms but despite my frequent travels for work, I was present at the birth of all my children. Interesting that the moyle was at our wedding and gave his card - little did I know how soon I would be calling him - and he was still around to handle Doug's *bris* as well.

Now with two babies, we were very crowded in our apartment,

Doug's bar mitzvah

so we decided to look for a house.

Shortly after Doug's birth, in 1961, we found a brand new house in Mayfield Heights, a new development attracting a lot of Jewish couples our age. The house was selling for $19,900 and only required $1900 down. We wound up purchasing it and scraped together enough money for a down payment. Fortunately, Barb's parents bought for us the appliances we would need so could move into this new house.

Since this was a new house it required a lot of things that one takes for granted, such as drapery rods and carpeting. Barb would vacuum the concrete floor to keep it from being too dusty. The house had no grass in the front and backyard and I took on the job of rototilling and planting grass; I must say, we had a nice lawn. The house may have been lacking in some amenities, but it was more spacious than our apartment, and we were also happy about the schools nearby for our children.

One of the extras this house came with was a basement entrance at the same level as the back yard. This gave me an idea that if I had a desk down there, I could see clients in the house. I proceeded to build a desk, using a door for the top and making cabinets from 1x2 wood furring strips that I covered with wall paneling. I made doors out of the same paneling and after a lot of finishing and sanding, it looked like a very nice desk. I placed the desk where the door to the outside would make it very convenient for clients to enter and meet.

After this project I divided the basement into sections with 2x4 and paneling, so in addition to an office, we also enjoyed a recreation area where I also built a bathroom and shower, using some tips from a bricklayer client. The rest of the project included carpentry, electrical, plumbing and painting I did myself with the help of a book from Home Depot: "Home Improvement Guide." I'm happy to say, the only electrocution I ever suffered was when I was a child!

After the first winter in the house we decided that we needed a garage since scraping the ice each morning off the car was a problem. This job I hired out! None of the homes in our development came with garages, but fortunately a local company came around to build garages and we got ourselves a two and a half car garage, including cement pad and apron, for $1,500. This may not sound like a lot of money now, but to make the payments for our new garage, we took out a 5-year loan, which was a big commitment for us at time. It was a good decision, and not only in the wintertime. It is the sidewall of the garage where my son learned how to play baseball; I would pitch to him using the garage as the backstop. He never got tired and just wanted to keep going - I guess that is why he wound up in the Beachwood softball hall of fame!

Soon after we moved in, our young son Doug broke his leg when he was going out the front door; his leg got caught between the screen door and front door and he twisted his leg, which caused a fracture of his tibia (shin). He went into a cast and it wasn't easy on him or Barbara, but kids heal fast. He wore a cast for several weeks, but managed to get around like any active toddler. He was back on his feet, literally, in a short amount of time.

While we were living in this house one of Barb's uncles was trading in his car and he asked if we wanted to buy a second car. The car was a Studebaker Lark. We bought it - but Barb thought the car was so funny looking she never wanted to drive it, so I ended up driving it to work about ten miles away!

Our daughter Lisa was born

We lived in this house for five years and our daughter Lisa was born while living there on May 27, 1963, which means my wife was taking care of three kids born in five years, while I was mostly gone and working. Luckily we lived in a wonderful neighborhood for the kids who had lots of friends. And fortunate for me, my wife was an amazing dedicated mother! The most exciting thing was that we had a daughter after having two boys. We felt that our daughter completed our family.

In Chapter 13, I'll take you from the beginning to end of my productive and prosperous career in accounting. I give Barb a lot of credit for raising our fine children while I was busy working – because as you'll read, I was pretty much always busy working!

Lisa's confirmation with grandfather Julius Gelfand and wife Rose

Visit to Niagra Falls with the kids and my dad

Josie, 1967 - 1983

CHAPTER 12

Raising Young Adults & Enjoying Our Grandchildren

The nice thing about giving birth to three kids within five years is that you get the pleasure (and challenge) of raising three teenagers all at the same time too! As it turns out, all three of our children not only turned out great, but joined my business as well.

From 1966 – 1975, we lived in a house on White Road, in University Heights. The house was a colonial with 3 bedrooms upstairs and 2 ½ bathrooms. We chose this location because we thought this would be the best school system for the kids. It turned out to be a good choice for this and many other reasons, such as good neighbors and eventually being very near my office. I did not have the desire to do improvements like I did in my previous house. I was very preoccupied at work, having several offices to go to. Sherman my partner and I were putting in so many hours at the office we would sometimes kid each other that we might meet one another in the middle of the night as he would be leaving the office about 2 am and I would be coming in about 4am!

I wasn't always working though. During this period of time we took many vacations with our children during summer break. One of our favorite places was Miami Beach Florida, where we stayed at the Newport Hotel on the beach after driving down from Cleveland. On one of those vacations we rented a water ski boat even though I had very little experience with boats, let alone water skis. Lee and Doug took to it like a fish to water; Lisa at this point was too young but she did it when she got older.

We lived on White Road for nine years and I somehow found the time to make some improvements in the basement. I built toy boxes across one wall with lids that opened in three sections. I also put down a vinyl floor in the room where I built the toy boxes. It was while I was cutting the tiles that Lee came by wanting to help and cut his thumb so badly with a utility knife that we rushed him to the hospital, requiring stitches. It took quite some time to heal. Like father, like son. I too suffered a serious accident (the electrocution) while trying to help my father!

While we were raising our children on White Road, our boys celebrated their bar mitzvah and Lisa was confirmed at Heights Temple which we joined in 1964 so that Lee could begin Hebrew classes. Heights Temple was our compromise since I was raised Orthodox and Barb was raised Reform; Heights Temple was Conservative, middle of the road for us.[1] We attended the High Holidays there for many years, first joining the temple as a young couple participating in the YPC (Young Peoples Congregation), and then moving up to the senior congregation, as we got older. I was quite active in the temple, becoming a board member for a while, but giving up my position

[1] Early on Barb and I had to find a way to compromise on a synagogue. With her background in Reform and mine in Orthodox, Conservative Judaism was the answer and we raised the kids accordingly. When we first married, we wanted my parents to feel comfortable eating in our home, so we set up a kosher household. But my folks still weren't comfortable eating in our home, and Barbara had a hard time with the whole system, so when my parents moved to California, we abandoned our kosher practices.

on the board when I was turned off by internal politics circulating around. Ultimately, we were members of Heights Temple for over forty years. We gave up our temple membership about 2010 since we were mostly in Florida during the Jewish holidays.

When we moved to White Road, we decided to get a dog and purchased a black miniature poodle from a breeder when the puppy was only a few weeks old and partially house trained. We took her home and named her Josie and in no time we had her trained. We discovered that this sweet dog could do real damage if she wasn't caged up when left alone. One day when we were leaving the house one of the kids put her in the cage, but when we got home she was waiting for us at the front door. We asked the kids if they put her in the cage and they assured us they did. We put her in the cage again and made sure the locking device on the cage was secure. The same thing happened again! Josie was at our feet by the front door. We then did it the third time and found out that she pushed the locking lever up with her thin nose to open the gate and free herself!

We eventually figured out that Josie was a wonderful dog as long as we gave her free reign of the house and didn't try to confine her to a cage. You could leave food on the coffee table and she wouldn't touch it unless you told her it was okay. She lived a very long life in dog years – sixteen years – until she succumbed to cancer. It was very painful for us to put her down, but we had no choice at the end of her life. It was a big adjustment for us all to learn to live without Josie. We tried a couple of dogs but having small grandchildren proved to be difficult to get the right fit.

During the years we were living in this neighborhood, I had the opportunity to reach back into my athletic passions, to play softball in the Beachwood softball league. The games were close by and I was eager to join, but here was one slight problem: you had to be at least thirty to play in this league. I wasn't going to be thirty until July 8, 1966, but the league started in June. The baseball commissioner made an exception in my case and this began my twenty-year career as an amateur softball superstar! My sons joined me after graduating

1975 Beachwood softball. I am front right

from college as the age restriction was changed to twenty-one if a parent was playing. Barb and Lisa were regularly there as the loyal fan club watching us play! Beachwood softball league was a summer league playing on Sunday mornings in the local neighborhood.

While I was managing this team and Lee and Doug were playing, one of my clients, Larry Adelman, was also managing a team with his son Todd. They were also exceptionally good players, but we never wound up playing with each other, since Larry and I were always captains.

Each year the commissioners of the league inducted star players into the Beachwood Baseball Hall of Fame. Lee was inducted the first year, and I was inducted the following year with my friend, Burt Curtis.

In 1980 I managed one of the teams and I drafted my son Lee who just graduated from college, to my team.[2] Well the season ended and we won the championship! Lee found his niche in hitting to right field and wound up leading the league with a 723 batting average, and of course, his fielding at shortstop was one of the best. When Doug graduated from college he also became a member of my team and we had all three Friedman men playing on our team. It was wonderful playing every Sunday morning with my boys. I retired from the league in 1992, concentrating more on golf and tennis,

[2] When we drafted players all the managers got together and selected from a pool of players that signed up to play. Certain players such as relatives were placed on the roster according to their ability. In Lee's case I told the managers that he was a great fielder but not a great hitter and therefore he went in the second and not the first.

which I played often at our club Oakwood, but Lee and Doug p for many more years.

White Road was a small street of only twenty houses, and we made many friends there. It so happened that our next-door neighbors also had a little girl Lisa a little bit younger than our Lisa. We were so close – literally – one night their Lisa was crying, and since her bedroom window faced our Lisa's bedroom, we thought it was our Lisa who was crying! Annually our street had a picnic at one of the homes. Our neighbors across from us were Holocaust survivors and kept a kosher house; they would ask the person hosting the picnic what they were grilling and she would buy the same thing, only kosher, and bring it in tinfoil to be put on the grill!

Although after nine years, we decided to move to a new community, Barb and I and the kids have many fond memories of being a part of the White Road neighborhood. The school system started deteriorating in our neighborhood and we decided to move for the sake of the children's education.

Moving to Pepper Creek

With the encouragement of my client, Mr. Cyncynatus, we purchased a lot in Pepper Pike community. Mr. Cyncynatus, for whom I still worked every Thursday night, was a painting contractor and he was painting several homes on this street. He suggested to me we should buy a lot on this street and put up a house.

It was quite an experience getting into this new house on Pepper Creek Drive, In Pepper Pike, Ohio. We built it from scratch, on a lot that was on a cul-de-sac. We had a little over an acre to our lot with the back yard that was heavily wooded with big trees.

After anguishing about such a major undertaking, we purchased a lot and had one of my clients who built homes put up the house. We had an architect draw plans and when we found out the cost we had him cut back on the size of the house. Later it turned out that we put up two additions to the house. Building the new house gave me a new job as before going to work I would go to the construction site and make sure that everything was going well.

We moved into our new house in May 1975.

A year after we moved into the house in 1976, I had a client who built in-ground pools and he built us a pool in our backyard for an excellent price. We situated the pool close to the house in order not to have to cut down so many trees. Shortly after that we added to the house in order to have a bathroom and dressing room for the pool. After we moved into the house I divided the basement into sections, paneled the walls, and added lighting and a vinyl floor. I also installed the lighting outside of our house, extending down each side of our long driveway. I was somewhat leery working with electricity after my boyhood electrocution accident. At this juncture I could afford to have this work done by professionals but I enjoyed doing this kind of labor and I got lot of pleasure out of it, so I did most of it myself.

As our sons grew older, they learned how to drive and purchased cars of their own. We expanded our two-car garage to make room for three cars. On top of the new garage we enlarged the master bedroom upstairs and the master bath. Our annual office picnic was held at our house with everybody coming casually in bathing suits and we provided some outdoor grilled foods. Our home and pool provided the perfect setting for this party.[3]

After we moved to Pepper Pike, we were all happy about the move except Lee because he was going into the 12th grade and didn't want to start a new school. No child wants to move school districts in their senior year, and Lee was no exception. He wanted to remain in the Cleveland Heights school district but even though we offered to pay tuition, the school district would not allow it.

It took some convincing at first, but Lee did transfer to Orange High School just for his senior year, and to his credit, he made it a very positive experience. He was a star soccer player so they were very happy to have him on the team and he made a lot of new friends.

[3] Our office also had an annual after-tax party usually held in the party room of a nice restaurant. This party was usually a highlight and everyone would attend and have a good time.

Our dream home in Cleveland under construction

Our dream house completed. 1975

Our winter backyard

The move turned out for the best for everyone in our family. When we moved to Pepper Pike, Doug and Lisa were starting junior high and high school respectively and they did not object to the move. All of the kids made a lot of good friends and received an excellent education.

Barb and I also enjoyed an active fulfilling social life with neighbors and friends our age. On Pepper Creek we made good friends with our next-door neighbor, the Friedmans. They introduced us to Stan and Carol Davis who played an important part in our lives as described in later chapters.

When Lee and Doug started driving, they both found jobs. Lee worked in a men's clothing store, at first stocking the store and then sales, which he seemed to enjoy. Doug started washing windows at people's homes and pretty soon the word got around and he had to hire a friend to help him since he was so busy. When he went off to Tulane he was able to sell the business, but the buyer did not pay him the full amount that they agreed to.

When Lee graduated Orange High in 1976, he left to attend Ohio State, which was about two hours away from our home, so we still saw him frequently. Lee enrolled at Ohio State with the intention to play on their college soccer team, but soon he turned soccer down. His reasoning was that the players were too strong and big, and he didn't want to compete with them. I have my own theory - the real reason was that he had a girlfriend (whom he eventually broke up with), and he wanted to spend more time with her then on the practice field of soccer. It was a big disappointment for me since I thought I could live my life through him, but then again, I also dropped my commitment to soccer in part because I had met Barbara and wanted to spend more time with her, so I wasn't one to judge!

Lee graduated from Ohio State in 1980, with an accounting degree. He came to work right out of college for our firm Friedman and Leavitt and after the required time became an accomplished CPA.

Doug entered Orange High School in 9th grade, and graduated from there in 1979. He then chose to break from the family tradition of Ohio State and attend college at Tulane University. While he was a student there, he threw me a curve ball when I got a call from him telling me that he wanted to join Sigma Chi fraternity. I tried to talk him out of it and told him that Lee was president of ZBT and he would be a legacy at Tulane if he joined ZBT, but he wouldn't hear of it. Even though I threatened not to pay his tuition, he prevailed and joined Sigma Chi. It turned out to be an excellent experience for him and he made many friends there, especially after finishing his schooling.

Doug transferred after two years to Case Western Reserve in Cleveland, where he continued his involvement with Sigma Chi, making good friends and meeting influential people. He graduated from Case Western Reserve in 1983. Instead of joining our firm right away, as his brother did, he instead went to work for a national accounting firm for a few years where he got some good experience that he brought to Friedman and Leavitt in 1986.

Lisa attended Orange High School for all four years, and was active as a cheerleader. She got the family gene of being smart with numbers and decided to major in finance at Ohio State and graduated from there in 1985. This skill could have gotten her a job just about anywhere but she made a very smart decision – she joined Friedman and Leavitt of course after she graduated!

Our children's marriages and our grandchildren

All three of our children had Jewish weddings officiated by a Rabbi under the chuppah and with the seven blessings. Our children follow the Jewish tradition much like their parents, which is very important to me.

Lee married Barbara on August 1 1982 (so now we have two Barbara Friedmans in the family). Doug married Ilene on September 22 1985. Lisa married Shelby on October 9 1994. Both my daughters-in-law, as well as my daughter attended Ohio State University and were full-time stay-at-home moms once the children came, with the exception of doing some part time work. Lisa did not get married until much later so she did work full time at Friedman and Leavitt. Since all my children were working for me, Barb would comment that she had the kids when they were young and now I have them. I enjoyed having them as much as she did. When we were working together in the office we would all walk to Jacks Deli (formerly Leftons) and have lunch together. What a treat for me.

Lee and Barbara

All three of our married children now live in Cleveland. (One of the benefits of employing them in my accounting firm – they all stay close to one another). When Barb and I come up North, it's easy for us to visit them all in Cleveland. It's always hard to leave Florida, but they make it worth it!

As a young adult I would often think, that since I was an only child until the age of 17, when I had my own family, I would like to have six children. I realized that after our third child was born, six children would not be economically practical. But now that our children have each married, my dream of having six children has become a reality, because my son and daughters-in-law are as close to me as family can be.

At this writing, I must be getting older, because our oldest son, Lee, is getting close to sixty himself! Lee and his wife, Barbara had known each other since elementary school. Their lives came together again as young adults, and in 1983 they were married. Barbara is much more outgoing than Lee ever was and has complemented Lee in everything that he does and what they have done together. Lee and Barbara raised our grandchildren, Aly and Zak.

Doug's marriage to Ilene DIck

Doug married his wife Ilene in 1985. Our daughter in law, Barbara introduced Doug to Ilene. Ilene has added a more serious and thoughtful side to Doug's adventurous nature and together they have found a common ground and made a very fulfilling life together. Doug at fifty-four may be the "younger brother" but he is very much an adult, raising with his wife Ilene our grandchildren, Samantha and Jared.

Lisa, now fifty-two, is married to Shelby, a hairdresser with his own hair salon in Beachwood, Ohio. They married in 1994 and gave us our grandchildren, Olivia and Julian who are both in high school. Shelby added a whole new dimension to our family. Lisa had always been serious about life; when she met Shelby, who was one of six

Daughter Lisa being wed to Shelby Hersh

children, she lightened up her attitude and became a lot more fun to be with. Shelby is a kind, fun loving guy who has endeared himself to our entire family. He is extremely handy and we've called upon his skills when making renovations to our various properties. Ilene and Barb and I get our hair done by Shelby.

I am so proud of my children who have grown to be so responsible and have chosen such good mates.

Our delightful grandchildren

We have a total of six grandchildren, and each of our kids had a boy and a girl.

Of course I will admit our first grandchild Alyson received considerable amount of attention from Barbara and myself. We saw Aly as often as possible, as we lived nearby to each other. We watched Alyson grow up through her acting career which included going to many plays starting in grade school including

Aly's Bat Mitzvah with father, Lee

when she got the lead role of "Annie." Subsequent roles earned her a professional equity card and she has been on stage in several cities including New York.

Aly and her husband Dr. Aaron Viny propelled me into the fantastic club of great grandpa when she brought baby girl Lilah Bea into the world this year. They live in New York. Aly is taking a sabbatical from her acting career where she has received her actor's equity card and has been in several plays after graduating from Ithaca University.

Samantha's Bat Mitzvah

Our next grandchild Samantha turned out to be a beautiful tall young lady who followed in the footsteps of her father and grandfather in becoming an accountant. She graduated from Ohio University and works in Cleveland for a national accounting firm. When growing up, Samantha had a passion for horses and won several blue ribbons for riding. Samantha once gave her parents a big scare when the shoe fell off the horse she was jumping, but all turned out well.

Zak's Bar Mitzvah

Our next grandchild Zak was a very cuddly young child who developed into a very interesting young man who can entertain most adults with the words that come out of his mouth. He is very knowledgeable in sports and business. Zak is a graduate from

University of Arizona and working in sales in Chicago, he's doing very well, capitalizing on his magnetic personality.

Jared's Bar Mitzvah

Then came Jared, our Army ranger. As a young man he was very creative - we used to call him "Farmer Friedman", as he grew vegetables in the garden around his house. He also was very into cooking, which his father Doug took over and has become quite a chef. Jared graduated from Ohio University and is an officer in US Army Elite Forces the Rangers, currently stationed in Afghanistan. Our prayers go out to him that he returns to us safely!

Julian's Bar Mitzvah with his father and his two grandfathers who both are holocaust survivors

Next came Julian. He amazes me - he has sculptured his body into a figure that has even earned him some modeling work while still a high schooler as a result of his stunning physique.

Our youngest grandchild, Olivia is also following in the footsteps of Alyson, our first grandchild, as she is also into acting and like Aly, has also played the lead in Annie, and in other school plays.

We have always entertained the kids at our club in Cleveland as

Olivia's Bat Mitzvah

well as bringing them to Florida and showing them a good time. Zak and Jared were good golfers and they often play with me at Oakwood in Cleveland and at the Polo club in Florida while Barb usually entertains the girls in both places. (I can gloat over the fact that when I had Zak down at the Polo club in Florida he got an eagle, which is like hole-in-one, on one of the courses here.)

The memories we have collected over the years of joyous times with our grandchildren could fill a book many times larger than this one. Without question, my greatest joy in life, alongside my marriage of almost sixty years to Barbara, comes from our three children, and their spouses, who have very much become like children to Barbara and me, and the most amazing grandchildren – and now great-grandchild – any grandpa could ever hope for. It is really for them, that I am writing this book.

WHERE I'M FROM
by Olivia Hersh

I am from three Holocaust survivors
from a woodworker who loves to farm and laugh
and a stay at home mother of six
I am from an accountant with a rough past
and a lady who has too many purses
and who knows a little about a lot
I am from the best hairdresser in the world
and the most caring and loving woman there is
I am from a family of four
one mom, one dad, and one brother too many

I'm from singing, dancing, and acting
from a world of creativity
from laughter and smiling
to the simple joy of helping

I am from nature
from the weeping willow and the evergreen
from the sycamore to the oak
to the elm and the maple
but I am most proud to be
on the most special tree,
my family tree

Poem written by Olivia to her Holocaust survivor grandparents

Daughter Lisa and I on one of our cruises

Lisa practicing for her cheerleading with Josie keeping her company

Lisa with Doug's friend's horse

Visiting California- Back row - Lee, my father, Doug.
Front row - Cousin Peter, Lisa and Barb

Doug's graduation from Case Western Reserve University

Lee at Ohio State with the rug he made hanging on the wall

Lee, Lisa, and Doug

Lee graduating from OSU

Proud father flanked by his sons Doug and Lee

Lisa graduation from OSU

Lisa's bridal shower with Alyson and three of her college roommates

Lee and Barb's wedding

Lisa and Shelby

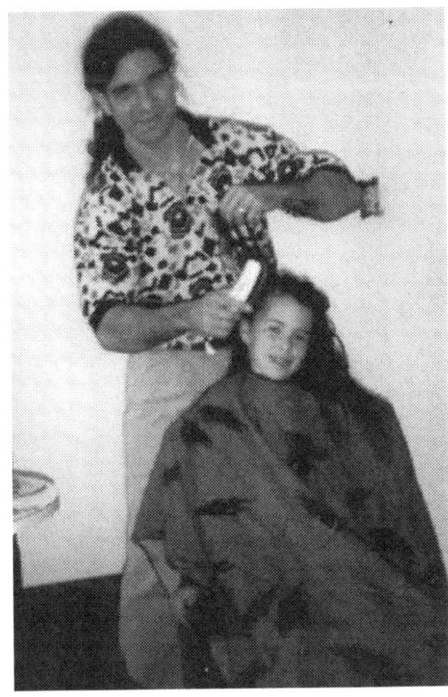

My son-in-law Shelby cutting my niece's hair

CHAPTER 13

My Accounting Career

After graduating from Kent State I continued to work for Mr. Kaplan's public accounting office on a full time basis.

As soon as I graduated, my parent's next-door neighbor, Mr. Treuhaft asked if I would do his accounting. He was a residential homebuilder and required some complicated accounting, which I was concerned about being able to do. I accepted his offer and was able to handle this type of accounting. Having this kind of knowledge enabled me to get this kind of business in the future. Coincidentally this builder built my home in Pepper Pike 15 years later.

I continued getting new accounts and my biggest source of new clients was my father-in-law who knew lot of business people and was always referring them to me. The only account I couldn't get was his, until the man that was doing his accounting died. The explanation for this is that the accountant did not charge him, plus he gave my father-in-law a present at holiday time. This was due to my father-in-law doing many favors for him.

As soon as I became an accountant I began acquiring clients

and working on them in my spare time. Even though the accounting jobs I held all required a lot of time I managed to be able to do both. The jobs I held permitted doing work on the side. Think of it as a professor who tutors in the evenings!

Our next-door neighbor was an attorney whose father managed a local CPA office and he suggested that I interview with him. Before accepting a position with this new firm I discussed it with Mr. Kaplan. He advised me that the company was a more prestigious CPA firm and he gave me his blessings to take the job.

I obtained the job there. He had some very prestigious clients but I was not happy with the people who were working there and the extreme frugality of the office. (For example, after I was hired, they told me to go to the local bookstore and buy my own red and blue mechanical pencil! Then I was told not to tear off the adding machine paper but let it accumulate on floor and turn it inside out so it could be reused! None of this sat well with me. Within a few months I decided to leave this firm, which for obvious reasons I've chosen not to name. Being unhappy in this job, I began searching for a new position.

I got an offer from a national accounting firm Haskins & Sells. When I started working for them I stopped working my weekend job at Alberts Deli since it wasn't very compatible with my profession. I did maintain my Thursday night job and got someone to work for me while I was traveling. And since I was home most weekends, I was able to service my accounts. You are getting the picture though, of the long hours I put in, in my professional life!

My career started with Haskins & Sells in their downtown Cleveland location and parking was at my expense. Since we had only one car Barb would occasionally drive me to the rapid transit, if she needed a car during the day to take Lee to the doctor or run some errands. My first annual Christmas party, complete with shrimp cocktail I couldn't imagine choking down, came around in lieu of bonuses. At this point, we weren't very religious, but I had been raised kosher and there was no way I was eating shrimp. I came up with a plan. When Barb finished hers I quickly changed her empty glass for mine and nobody knew the difference.

I was the token Jew at the firm and when we went to companies that had Jewish ownership or management I was usually included in the assignment. From time to time I would encounter anti-Semitism. One memorable day we were on an audit of a General Motors Fisher Body in Cleveland. One of the senior accountants and I were on a coffee break. My coworker and I were standing at the coffee dispensing machines having a cup of coffee and the comptroller of the GM plant came by and got himself a cup from the vending machine. He asked my coworker and me about the big holiday the Jews were celebrating tomorrow. My partner wisely turned to me and asked, "What is the Jewish holiday you are celebrating tomorrow?" I answered Rosh Hashanah, the Jewish New Year. With that answer the comptroller scampered off with his tail between his legs and made himself invisible for the remainder of the audit.

One of my jobs included doing an audit in Scranton, Pennsylvania, when the Erie and the Lackawanna railroads merged. For two months, I was in Scranton all week, only coming home on weekends. Interestingly our first trip to Scranton was by a small commuter plane and this was going from a small airport called Burke Lakefront airport; this flight made me very nervous because this was my first flight on a plane. They were defrosting the plane, the whole wing was ice and there was snow everywhere.

The rest of the trips to Scranton were by train. We would leave Cleveland Sunday night and be in Scranton ready for work Monday morning, shaving and showering on the train. Returning to Cleveland we would leave Friday evening and be home Saturday morning, so I wasn't even home the full weekend. The last two weeks of the job we had to spend two weeks in Scranton without going home. Of course this kind of commitment was very hard on Barb who was home with the children.

In the almost three years I was working for Haskins & Sells, I acquired a lot of invaluable experience. Barb and I decided I needed to find an alternative that wouldn't require me to travel so much.

I found a new job with Baden & Linden CPA's, another local CPA office, which had approximately 10 employees and two partners and did require travel out of the city. The atmosphere there was much better and I stayed there for five years getting some very valuable experience before I went out on my own. I was able to put together my experience with the larger accounting firm and with a local CPA firm to have good knowledge of being able to handle small and large clients and do audits as well.

Throughout my career I was accumulating clients always with my employer's knowledge that I was doing so. I supplemented the amount of work that I had by offering my services to CPA's who needed one or two days help. This is how I started out my practice.

My office was at home and I would meet clients at my home as I was building up my accounts, when a wonderful thing happened that lasted almost forty-five years.

One of my wife's good friends, Eileen indicated to my wife that her brother-in- law, Sherman Leavitt, had just started an accounting practice and was working out of his house. We were introduced to one another and we liked what each of had to offer. After numerous conversations, we decided to become business partners. In the summer of 1968 we rented a small office - one room with a wooden partition down the middle and each of our desks on one side of the partition. By August of that year we became full partners.

We met with great success, and soon outgrew this humble beginning. Over the years, we grew to four offices: Cleveland, Painesville, Elyria[1] and Canton. We hired a secretary bookkeeper for each office except for the Canton office where it was not needed.

[1] One day Sherman and I went to the Elyria office and we went out to lunch to a Big Boy restaurant. I was busy looking at some papers and when the waiter asked me what I wanted, I said, "I'll have the same." When I got my meal I bit into the hamburger and realized it had cheese on it. This was the first time that I had ever mixed milk with meat in a meal. Years later I also ate shrimp, bacon and ribs. Now, I eat any delicious food that comes my way, although I still have an appreciation for the traditions that were dear to my father.

As our accounting practice grew we moved to larger quarters. In 1975 we purchased our own 5000 square feet building in Cleveland. (Moving into our own building was an excellent move for us, but it did come with one loss. Our previous office was across the hall from two independent jewelers who repaired and set diamonds for wholesale customers and their own customers. Leonard was an American and Henry was an Auschwitz survivor. I became very friendly with both of them and ate lunch with them almost on a daily basis. In 1974 the restrictions for buying or selling gold were removed and gold was available to anyone at a very low price. I purchased a four-ounce piece of gold from Leonard and I cut out a small piece from this bar and made an initial be to be worn around my wife's neck. Leonard helped me make it just perfect. Leonard moved to Arizona and Henry became a good client of mine; he opened his own jewelry store in addition to his ongoing setting and repairing jewelry business.)

At first, we leased out part of the building but eventually, as our staff grew, we used all of the building ourselves. Our clients ranged from a milk man with a milk route to a strip coal mine that had a helicopter, which sometimes picked us up and brought us back to their office in Marietta, Ohio about 175 miles away. (One day as we were flying practically over our house the pilot landed the helicopter on our front lawn. I got out of the helicopter and my wife who was standing nearby got on and joined my son Lee who was already on the helicopter. They flew to the airport where Lee and I left our cars).

Client's helicopter dropping me off after the day of working for at the coal mine office in Marietta

Sherman and I were very compatible business partners. What made the partnership work was that we complemented one another. Even though we had disagreements, mostly involving our kids, we always resolved it. I was good at setting office procedures and hiring employees and Sherman was very bright and made friends very easily, resulting in getting new clients. Over the years, we both had to deal with some serious medical issues. We individually, and as a partnership, had some hard times, but we really prospered together.

Our accounting practice was growing since we gave good service and we hired good people (the best of which were our children who did excellent work for our clients. We treated our help fairly and they became long-term employees. I did most of the hiring for the firm, and some of those employees were with us for more than twenty-five years. Of about twenty staff employed, over fifty percent of them were CPAs, which in the world of accounting firms, was considered a very good ratio. Some of the non-CPA's conducted themselves in such a professional way, we almost considered them as CPA's because of the kind of work that they were doing.

Joanne was with us for over twenty-five years before she retired in 2002. She became my right-hand person. She started with us as a typist and because she had gone to business school, she was able to work her way up to doing complex accounting tasks. She was adept at taking dictation and improvising the letters that I dictated. Kathy was another woman who has been with us for over twenty-five years and is still working for the firm; her skills honed at Friedman & Leavitt enabled her to be invaluable for one of our largest clients.

My star decision in hiring came when we were looking for a CPA and I interviewed two CPAs and I could not come to the conclusion of which one to hire. I consulted with my partner Sherman and we decided to hire both of them. These men turned out to be excellent employees and have been with the firm for many years.

My partner Sherman helped orchestrate the purchase of another accounting firm in 1980. Even though we paid a steep price for this practice, it turned out to be a very wise purchase, because they came with quality accounts that had great potential to grow.

The business continued to grow. We hired more employees and moved the Elyria and Canton practices to Cleveland since we could make more money by staying in our Cleveland office. Both Sherman and I had homes relatively close to our office, which made things easier. By the early eighties, I found it wonderful to have all three kids working with me as they were great employees and I didn't have to worry about them doing anything negative to the company. More often they were influential in getting new business. Once in awhile personalities entered the picture involving family issues that would have to be responded to and resolved. But nothing came up that we couldn't work out; all in all, it was a truly rewarding experience for all of us.

The 1980s brought the purchase of the accounts of another CPA who had a nice practice, which included auto dealerships. We did a good job for these auto dealers and consequently we were able to get many new dealerships. In fact, one of those dealerships we acquired grew to over twenty dealerships, and we continued to handle all of the accounting and taxes for this owner, including providing him certified audits that drew from my experience earlier in my career. Eventually my son Lee took over the audits and put a team from our office together and would specialize in doing these audits.

When our sons came into the business, (Lee in 1980, Doug in 1986, and David, my partner's son in 1981[2]) we were able to grow even more, especially into our specialty of handling automobile dealerships.

I'd visit each dealership on a monthly basis and bring work back to our office for completion. In the beginning of our work with the dealerships, our sons were still in school and of no help. My load at

---

[2] Lee joined us right from college and then earned his CPA license. Doug worked for a national accounting firm where he earned his CPA license before joining our firm. Lisa came to us straight out of college. Sherman's son David came straight from college to work for us and soon became a CPA. Sherman's son Joel also joined our firm.

work had increased to the point that I could not fit all my clients into my monthly calendar. At this point Sherman suggested that I turn over some accounts to him. Then, our son Lee was ready to join the practice and he started going with me to the auto dealers. When he gained experience I let him go to many accounts on his own. We followed the same training protocol for our son Doug. While achieving success in our business, Doug became president of the east side CPA Association due to his hard work in getting speakers for monthly meetings that most CPA's attended.

After several years with our firm Doug decided to go into the coffee business as he saw that to be a great future. After working a few years in the coffee business he determined that it was too competitive and not much money could be made at it. He came back to the firm and continued being an accountant. My partner Sherman and I made annual gifts to our sons so that they would eventually have enough shares to be equal partners. When Doug left the firm I gave him a lot of money and he relinquished his stock back to me. When he came back from the doomed coffee business, the stock he gave up was no longer available. It was allocated among the four partners with no transfers permitted, thus Doug became a valuable employee with responsibilities and a very good salary, but no equity. Still, since his name was on the door, clients felt he was a partner.

A short detour back in history: Doug wasn't the only family member who tried his luck at a new venture, only to have to admit it wasn't working. In 1969, a client brought to us an invention that would allow snowmobiles to have wheels instead of skis on the front, so you could use the snowmobile in all kinds weather. It sounded really good to us and we proceeded to raise money from investors to purchase twenty snowmobiles, and then we signed up a couple of golf courses as clients.

Turns out, to be successful in the snowmobile business, you need snow, even with our modified snowmobiles. That year, the weather did not cooperate with our entrepreneurial ambitions. It was rainy and sloppy, instead of snowy, and that kind of weather didn't sit well with our snowmobiles. We even tried hauling by truck the snowmobiles to an alternate location where the ground was much better. Bottom line - this venture failed and we lost all our money. I felt really bad for the investors because some were friends and others were clients. I was glad that we limited each investor to $2,000.

Snowmobile with wheels for rental

The combination of the grueling hours and pressure of our accounting work, alongside our failing, snowmobile business, added by dark days of my youth still haunting me, led me to a serious depression that required medical treatment. A psychiatrist prescribed medication that helped bring me back to normal. Sherman and Barbara were my rock during this difficult time until I found my footing again. I'm happy to say that I was able to fully recover, and refocus on our accounting business.

As I look back on my long and prosperous career in the accounting field, I am very satisfied with the results and grateful that as I neared retirement, I was able to provide a livelihood for our three children as well.

Friedman &Leavitt offices, Howard & Joan visited Barb and I before they returned to California

My partner for over 40 years, Sherman Leavitt ,with his wife LeeAnn

Client mega auto dealer Tom Ganley and wife Lois

Paul Cyncynatus, one of my mentors, with Henrik Sperling

Client auto dealer, Dick Deacon and wife Carol

Lunch after golf at Oakwood Country Club with Mike Supler, Dave Robinson, Lee and me

My associates and clients

2015 lunch get together with Ed Weisler and Sheldon Lewin, associates at Baden & Linden

At the opening of the new Jack's Deli

CHAPTER 14

A Lot of Work, But Plenty of Play!

After reading about the development of what turned out to be a very successful accounting career, one could get the idea that I was a man who was what we might call "all work no play." Yes, I certainly put in the hours, as any accounting profession demands. However, Barb and I had a lot of fun together over our long marriage (and we still do). All work no play is for sure not our motto. With the family Barb and I took many trips to recreation parks, enjoyed family cruises to the Caribbean over the Christmas holidays, and engaged in many more enjoyable vacations.

And let me tell you about cards and me! We go way back.

My profession always demanded an enormous commitment of my time. But I did take time off.

The family would gather together at my Aunt Margaret's place on a monthly basis. The men would play Gin and the women would play Canasta. From watching my father play I learned the game of Gin.

I have many cousins in Cleveland and my Aunt Margaret organized a monthly family get together where the men played cards as well as the women at different homes each month. I participated when the games were in our house.

Much later in the mid '70s my friend Stan asked me if I would join the Monday night Gin card game. The game that they played on Monday nights at each other's houses was a six-man game and there was a lot of strategy involved. It took me quite awhile to learn the strategy of the game – my Gin playing experience helped. It proved to be a game that went on for many years. When some players dropped out over the years, we joined another group that has been playing for about twenty years. One of the players, an avid writer, even wrote a book about Gin, and while disguising names, wrote about us in his book.

The group continues till this day on Monday nights. The game isn't for large stakes but it requires skill to play well. The game has moved down to Florida in the winter months by again combining our group with another group.[1]

Barb and I would go to Las Vegas after tax season in May and there we would play Craps and Blackjack. On one of our first trips, both Barb and I were lucky and we wound up as winners. We've been going annually to Vegas for many years – sometimes we win, sometimes we lose. One time when Barb was winning at Blackjack and I had lost at the Craps table, it got to be pretty late and Barb did not want to quit as she was winning, so I went up to our room. When she returned to our room she was all-smiles - she did the best she ever has and won a tidy sum.

[1] My long-time friend, Larry is also a member of the Monday night Gin game that's played at each other's houses in Cleveland. About three years ago he and his wife Joanne purchased a home at the Polo Club in Florida near us. We expanded our card games to Florida, and Larry claims to hold the continuous record of 44 victories in Gin.

Being regular players in Vegas, Barbara and I receive many amenities such as restaurants and shows for free, not having to wait in line for shows and getting good seats with a little additional tipping.

In 1997, we joined my friend Stanley who owned a condo in Florida and invited us to spend a weekend with them. We did, and really enjoyed ourselves. Stanley decided to purchase a house at the Polo Club, and he wanted me to do the same. After we purchased a house in Florida in January 13, 1998, that became a retreat for our family as well. This home at the Polo Club is where we still reside for most of the year. Can't complain about living in sunny Florida, especially in the wintertime!

Since my parents and brother were in California, a sizeable distance from Cleveland, we did invest a bunch of time and money into making that journey about once a year. One memorable trip took place in 1962, when Barbara was pregnant with Lisa, and the boys were only age four and one. I don't know what we were thinking with our boys so young, but we boarded a train in Cleveland to Chicago, and then transferred to another train that took us to California. The weather in Chicago was extremely cold, but we weren't there for long. The whole journey took less than a week each way. We had a Pullman compartment with upper and lower bunks, which the boys thought was lots of fun. Barb slept in the lower bunk and I shared the upper bunk with the two boys, which means I probably didn't get much sleep! We brought lots of toys for them to play with, and they were very well behaved. It was worth the trip, as we were very happy to see our family.[2] We stayed with them for about nine days. Over the years, we traveled to California quite a bit, but that was the last of the long train rides. Going forward, we took an airplane! My parents would come in from California, mostly for special occasions, and I had a client as a travel agency who would send them airline tickets to pay for my accounting services.

The first time I visited Israel, in 1985, Barbara and I went with

[2] We always looked forward to seeing my parents and brother when they traveled out east for weddings and family bar mitzvahs.

my partner Sherman and his wife Leanne with a Jewish group on a tour bus. Naturally we visited all the sites and enjoyed every one of them. When I came to Yad Vashem my heart began to pound and I felt so elated to be there. I inquired from people working there about putting a tracer on my mother's whereabouts. I gave them all the information I had about my mother and they put it into the computer but sadly, we could find no trace of her. She was sent to the crematoriums with millions of other good Jews like herself.

I did notice one difference in being in Israel- my heart was relieved. I felt at ease, as opposed to when I went back to Slovakia in 1989 and was afraid to even ask someone about a building there. To this day the torment that I went through is still there and I'm afraid it will never go away. Maybe writing about my story in these memoirs will help with the healing process, but I've come to accept that some traumatic events like what I endured, you don't ever get over them – you just figure out how to live well despite them.

Another memorable trip in 1992 brought Barb and me back to Israel, this time to celebrate my Aunt Honor's 90th birthday. My cousin from New York, Lila, met us there for this occasion. Lila is five years my senior, an attorney whom I always looked up to. She wrote and spoke fluent Hungarian. Honor was one of my mother's sisters who immigrated to Israel before the war and married there. She had one child, Nechama, with her husband, David. My aunt who was very scholarly left Europe after graduating from college and her desire

Aunt Honor and me

was to go to medical school but the war disrupted everything. During the war years she was reduced to raising chickens on a small plot of land that they had. After the war she and her husband built a four-plex apartment on the property and one of the suites became their own. My aunt and her children were still living on this property when we visited them.

While we were in Israel we went on to see and visit family and sites there. My father's brother, Lazer and his entire extended family (which included three children and grandchildren) lived in the next community over, Ramat Gan, just outside of Tel Aviv. We met in the reception area of a nearby hotel since no one's home was large enough to accommodate our gathering, and I got to know much of the family.

I connected to first cousins close in age to Barb and me who were very nice, and whom we'd never met before. Barb and I visited many sites throughout Israel, including Masada, Dead Sea and the Wailing Wall, before traveling north up to Haifa to visit my first cousin Edith and her husband and family. I had fixated in my memory of Edith the picture of a blond, blue-eyed girl, so it was a surprise for me to find a married woman with a husband and two boys and a girl all serving in the Israeli army! We flew from Israel to Egypt and then from Egypt to Antalya, Turkey. The driver took us to the Istanbul coast, known as the Turkish Riviera. We saw many sights over the two day drive, visiting small cities and several tourist attractions famous for serving tea, while showing customers merchandise like Oriental Rugs.

One restaurant I remember in particular allowed us to pick out a fish from the pond, and then they grilled it for us. You don't get fish any fresher than that and I still remember how delicious it was. We toured the sites of Istanbul, before we flew by way of Paris (although never visiting Paris) and then back to United States. This trip was certainly one of the most spectacular trips of my lifetime with Barb.

The kids never accompanied us on our trips to Israel, but they got there their own way, and in fact, Lisa was even engaged to her husband Shelby on Mount Masada, as well as our granddaughter

Aly becoming engaged to Aaron in Israel. My cousin Nechama, who lives in Israel, was the first to be informed of Lisa and Shelby's engagement. I was so glad that they were able to visit with Nechama on their trip and also to meet Honor, Nechama's mother, who was 92! Nechama was so excited to be present for the engagement that she along with my cousin Lila met up to come to Shelby and Lisa's wedding six months after seeing her in Israel. So Israel holds a very special place in our family's hearts.

Besides plenty of family trips with our children, Barb and I have also spent a lot of time with other couples, playing golf and other activities at our club that we both really enjoyed, and still do.

My partner Sherman was a member of a couples club with friends of his from high school. They met monthly and socialized a lot, and Barb and I got to know many of them through Sherman. One day two of the couples, Dr. Jerry and his wife Elaine, and Jerry's sister Fran and her husband Bill, joined Sherman and his wife Leanne and Barb and me for an amazing trip to Europe. We rented an eight-passenger van and toured all over Europe. Bill was our designated driver and Sherman the navigator. We all hit it off so well, we became close friends and took many more trips together.

Barb and I also socialized and vacationed with my friend Mort from high school, who married Marcia, and raised three children. Mort and Marcia also became good friends with our couples group and joined us on several vacation trips.

Another notable trip we took: we, and three other families vacationed with all their children in New England. It took two vans following each other and making several stops along the way to get all of us from Cleveland to our destination!

Our second vacation with Sherman, his wife Leanne and their two boys and daughter, included my wife and I and our three children to the Host farm in Pennsylvania. We hauled a snowmobile on a trailer hitched to one of the cars that was a relic left over from the snowmobile business. When we started riding around the grounds of this resort all eyes were on us. And when we came into the lobby everyone was asking questions. We could have succeeded in that business if the weather only cooperated a little. We went home feeling good.

In Cleveland besides going out for dinner, and enjoying cultural events around town, we also developed another set of friends that centered on Oakwood Country Club. These friends expanded our friendship circle beyond the friends we'd made through Sherman and his wife. One of the friends in our couples circle, Stanley and his wife Carol, helped us join the club. Stanley was a salesman and owner of auto leasing company; I was his accountant. For my 50th birthday Stanley put in an application to the Oakwood country club as a birthday present and he sponsored me. (Oakwood is a private club and you have to be sponsored by a current member). Barb and the family were very happy that we joined. We were members of the club from 1986 until it closed in 2010. We participated in many activities, including plenty of golf and tennis. Oakwood country club friends became part of our social network, and our children also joined in and benefitted.

Truthfully, I could write an entire book just chronicling the trips that Barb and I, and sometimes the kids, have taken in the USA, Israel, and Europe. The point I want to make is this: Yes, I was, and have always been hard working. But also just as true: Barb and I have surrounded ourselves with a whole lot of fun friends, and we have made socializing and traveling a significant part of our life together. It balanced out the long days and has given us many good memories.

And finally, no chapter about our family life and the fun we've had would be complete if I didn't write about the special cars we have owned, well worth mentioning, as it has created many special family memories and given me much joy.

In 1972, my friend, Jerry, noticed a used car advertisement for a 1970 Porsche, and I had been looking for a car. He encouraged me to go look at the car. It was an orange 911T, only two years old and in excellent condition. Jerry, an obstetrician and a car buff, convinced me to buy the car and Barb was supportive.(Interesting twist – millions

1970 Porsche

of men have what's called a "mid-life crisis", feel younger, leave their wives, and buy a sports car. Here I was, lucky me, being encouraged by my wife to buy one!)

So we bought the car and Barb's instincts were correct - it brought both of us much joy.

I actually took the car to a local racetrack and hired professional drivers to teach me how to navigate the curves on the track. (In subsequent days I went out on the track myself but I found it was very difficult and I never entered any races.)

Barb, who could drive the Porsche since she learned to drive on a shift car, suggested that Lee should take his driver's test in the Porsche because it was easier to park than our other family car, a large Cadillac. So one day, she decided to teach Lee how to drive the Porsche. This is a teenage memory I bet Lee has never forgotten. Lee may be one of the few American teenagers ever lucky enough to brag to his friends that he passed his driver's test in a Porsche!

I was so happy with this car that in the winter I took off the hubcaps and stored them under our bed. But different than the long marriage I've enjoyed with Barb, that just gets better and better over time, we had to face the same dreaded loss we experienced when we lost our beloved dog. After four years, it was time to sell the car, because the undercarriage was rusting.

I was now hooked on owning a special car. I replaced the Porsche with a Citroen Maserati, a very unique car with beautiful lines and a hydraulic system that one could control from inside of the car that

1972 Citroen Maserati

would raise and lower the car. When this was happening all eyes were on the car. This was the car we've seen plunging slowly into water in a James Bond movie. I felt like a movie star!

I enjoyed the car but it came with a lot of mechanical problems. Luckily one of my clients was a dealership that handled it for me. Then one morning when I was driving to the office, the radio stopped working and I was trying to see what was wrong; I took my eyes off the road for a few seconds. That's all we needed for me to hit the car in front of me, doing minimal damage to their car, but sadly, doing considerable damage to my car. An architect in our building heard about the accident and he offered to buy the car from me, and to make the repairs himself. I sold him the car, and there ended my many years of feeling like James Bond. It was good while it lasted.

Tour group in Budapest,
Barb center front and I am behind her

Famous Dohani temple in Budapest with schedule of services. Actor Tony Curtis contributed to refurbishing

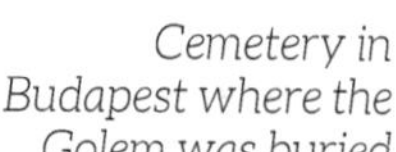

Cemetery in Budapest where the Golem was buried

Journey to Alaska with the Heimans and Weissenbergs

Barb and I by helicopter on glacier in Alaska

Barb with Israeli soldier on our trip to Israel

Dead Sea encounter in Israel, Barb and me in the center

Annual trip to Niagra on the Lake, Spevaks, Newmans, and us

Pushkin Museum in Russia

Moskva Russia with friends Paul an Harriet Dennis

In Russia, a cheder learning in a temple

In Greece, standing in front of the Parthenon

An Egyptian bazaar

Barb greeting children in Kenya. Background is the huts they live in

Kenya Africa Safari, in a vehicle used to observe animals

Tour of the orient, first stop Japan

Barb and I taking a rickshaw ride in Singapore

Hole in One!

L-Steve Schwartz, my cousin Herbie's son, member of the Parachute Express, two other members on the right

My corvette

Cars- Doug's, Lee's, Barb's, Les's

The not-to-be-missed annual Chanukah gathering in our home

CHAPTER 15

Retirement & Enjoying Family

Our Polo Club home was almost complete when we purchased it, and we just put some finishing touches on it. The Polo Club is a beautiful facility with two great golf courses, thirty-four tennis courts, spas, pools, exercise facilities and all the amenities we could ask for. We did have a pool put into the back yard of our home, as our grandchildren were little and the big pool wasn't as convenient at that time. It's really a beautiful place.

Right after we moved into the Florida house, when they were finishing the pool, the construction workers ran some extension cords through our side door living space between the threshold and door. Barb and I were standing nearby when we saw what appeared to be a rat run under the door and into the house. I went into the house and saw it run into the kitchen and into the cabinet. At this point we called the exterminator and he came out right away. He set some traps and told us to go out to dinner. When we got back from dinner the rat was in a trap, and the exterminator came back and disposed of the rat. While we were sitting in the den we could see a black little critter dart out of the kitchen cabinet. We immediately called the exterminator and he came out and told us the bad news that the rat had babies while under the cabinet - and they usually have seven babies. He set more traps while we stayed in the house and put towels under the doors to our bedroom. By morning most of the baby rats were caught, which I had to dispose of. Later that morning the seventh and last critter went in a trap. This was a harrowing experience that I tried to minimize with Barb because I was afraid that she would want to sell the house.

When we purchased our home in Florida we started vacationing in Florida for longer periods of time each year. Eventually I was living two weeks in Florida and two weeks in Cleveland during the winter. While in Florida I took work with me and made many phone calls and contacts while there, and when I came back from Cleveland for two weeks I worked sometimes eighty hour weeks trying to keep up with all the work.

We loved our vacation home, and although we have made some cosmetic improvements over the sixteen years that we have been here, we still look forward to returning in the fall after having been in Cleveland all summer.

We spent more time in Florida each winter until working and vacationing became harder and harder to manage. Once I retired, we became official Florida residents, spending the entire winter in Florida, and on summers and special occasions, returning to Cleveland.

My partners were not satisfied with this arrangement and were troubled by the time I was spending in Florida. All this tension was bothering me. Barbara and I decided that it wasn't worth getting so upset about this and it was time to set the stage for my retirement. After forty-five years in the accounting field, I decided once my sons were fully involved in the business to gradually go into retirement at age seventy on November 1, 2006, to be fully retired by 2009, when I would be seventy-three.

At this time we became official snowbirds – spending the entire winter in Florida and traveling up north in the summer, or for holidays and special occasions.

Unfortunately my partner Sherman passed away about a year after my retirement contract was signed. I felt great sadness at the loss of my long-time close friend and partner. About a year before he died, Sherman asked me to have my attorney prepare my retirement contract based on our verbal agreement, which I did. I presented the contract my attorney prepared to Sherman and he was in total agreement that this was our understanding. But then, Sherman's attorney made numerous changes to the contract, creating all kinds of problems and conflict.

I was not in a negotiable frame of mind. I was always under the impression that Sherman and I had an understanding, which we did, but his lawyer twisted his thinking. My son Lee who was one-quarter partner in the firm did not want to enter discussions or negotiations for the fear of alienating Sherman and his son. Eventually, I became so aggravated with the whole situation, I told Lee to communicate to Sherman that he could have it all his way. Lee tried to persuade me not to cave in, but I just wanted to be done with this whole dragged out negotiation. Therefore in 2006 we finalized the contract, which I feel didn't treat me fairly. I believe that they felt that I was walking away with a lot of money and were not sure that they would be able to pay me should there be a business downturn, but this turned out to be a non-issue. I was paid all that was owed to me before the end of 2010 and both of my sons are still employed with the firm, and the firm is doing extremely well.

As Barbara and I have settled into retirement, still enjoying one another's company, we love Florida, but we look forward to our summers with our family.

As I am writing this, we are making our seventeenth trip back home to Cleveland for the summer of 2015. We have been doing this journey every year except last year, 2014, when both Barb and I had back surgeries and we flew back and had the car shipped. I am happy to say that we were both well enough to drive to Florida this October 2015. We usually drive down in October and drive back in May. It's not a hard drive - we do it in two days, about sixteen hours of driving each way. Barbara and I share the driving and listen to books on tape. We did have one hair-raising incident on the highway when Barb was driving; there was a rock in the middle of the road and the rear tire hit it and exploded. Luckily she was able to pull over to the side of the road and we called for assistance. The SUV that we were driving had to be unloaded to get to the spare tire and we had our luggage, golf clubs and what have you, sitting on the side of the road while AAA took out the tire and replaced the one that blew out. Could have been a lot worse!! When we go back and forth from Cleveland for holidays or special occasions we fly.

Over the years we have made many friends in Florida with whom we golf and play cards with and we sadly say goodbye to them every May. The consolation is that we have good friends in Cleveland as well, and of course, the best part - our kids and grandkids live in Cleveland.

The three years of winding down before my full retirement prepared me well for my full retirement. The fact that I was very active in sports at this point, namely golf, and tennis, as well as an active card player, occupied the void left from working. I also continued to enjoy an active social life with Barb in the clubs we belonged to. Retirement gave me added time to enjoy my children and grandchildren's' company and their activities. Even though these things kept me busy, I found time to release my energy on some home improvements projects. As hard as I worked when I was working, I'm not one of those men who slips into boredom upon retirement, unable to let go of my life shaping around my work. I've never second-guessed my retirement, and I continue, till this day, to enjoy these years in my life very much.

It sure makes our life easier that when we come up from

Cleveland, as we can easily spend time with all of the family in one location. Lee and Lisa live in the same suburb called Orange Village within a couple of blocks of each other and our Cleveland home is just a five-minute ride to the next suburb. Doug lives only ten minutes away, in Mayfield Heights, Ohio. We conveniently live in the middle of these two locations.

All my kids own their homes, an accomplishment Barb and I were very instrumental in helping them achieve by giving them each the down payment they could use in buying their first home and then a second gift when they each upgraded to a new home.

It is true that working in the accounting field required many long hours away from home, but our children would agree that there were certainly benefits that we shared as they established their own families: none of our children were saddled with school loans to contend with, since Barb and I paid for all of their education, as well as the grandchildren's schooling as needed. This parental act gave me great joy, especially because, through no fault of my father, he was not able to do the same for me, and I was working all the time throughout high school and college to meet expenses. I know that my father would have given me the money if he could have, but he was an immigrant struggling himself. From my early days I could not get myself to ask my father for money since I always felt that I would be putting a hardship on him. Living in America, and achieving financial success in my chosen field, allowed Barb and I to share our good fortune with our children and grandchildren – it doesn't get better than that.

Growing older myself meant watching my parents age, and it wasn't easy with us in Florida and Cleveland, to be able to care for them. We were able to visit California to celebrate my dad's 80th birthday. I saw my dad several times after his 80th birthday, but ten years later, when we visited him to celebrate his 90th birthday, he was still "with it" but his eyesight was fading. He got around very nicely without any help or cane, but a few months after our visit, he had a major stroke, and my brother Marvin, who lived out by my parents warned me that if I visited, he wouldn't even recognize me. He went into a nursing home in a wheelchair and I'm so grateful that we visited him for his 90th birthday, because when I visited him at the nursing home, he was completely unresponsive. It was heartbreaking for me, especially when he didn't even know who I was. I returned to Cleveland with a heavy heart, and he passed a few weeks later, on June 13, 1997, unfortunately, on Marvin's birthday!

Within two years, my stepmother also passed away. Marvin and his wife Ann[1] and their two daughters continued their life in California. Marv's doctorate in pharmacy has surely come in handy when we've had any questions regarding medications for our aches and pains! He graduated from UCLA and USC and worked at the VA hospital where he put in twenty years and retired. He then started doing consulting work for setting up hospitals on their medical plans. Ann volunteers at The Reagan library where she is a docent. Their oldest daughter, Susan, is a patent attorney and their younger daughter Andrea just finished pharmacy school, following her dad's footsteps.

My brother Marvin and his wife Ann, although living across the country in California, have always been an integral part of my family. We never missed being together for celebrations as we would travel, with our families, to each others children's bar mitzvahs, and they came in for my kid's weddings. My family and Marv's family keep in close contact and I lucky to have their warm and kind presence even though distance keeps us apart physically.

The last time Barbara and I visited California was a surprise visit for Marv's 60th birthday on June 13, 2013. Marv and his family may live far away, but we are very grateful for our family connection. As Barb and I get older, we will surely be turning to him more often for

[1] Ann was born in Europe after the war and immigrated to Israel where she went to school. When Marv visited Israel our family was close to Ann's family and Marv and Ann got together and were married and moved to California. Ann spoke Hungarian as well as Hebrew and now English. I get to practice my Hungarian with her and Marv has learned a lot of Hebrew and Hungarian from her as well.

his pharmacy expertise!

My Mother's family - the seven of them - produced only five children: My cousin Lila the, attorney whom I was close with, passed away eight years ago. Her two daughters living in Connecticut got the family together at their home in 2013, which included the remaining three first cousins. I am the oldest; Nechama and her husband David came in from Israel and Peter the youngest came in from California with his wife Judy and daughter Lauren. It was a great get together, leading to the three of us being in Connecticut last year to celebrate Lila's granddaughters wedding.

I am very fortunate to be spending my retirement years still very much surrounded by family. My enduring marriage to Barb, my children and grandchildren, and the occasional get-together with extended family are really what gives me the most joy in my older years. As much as I got great satisfaction and prosperity from my career, and I still do appreciate many friendships that have giving our life great fun over the years, in the end, it's all about family and the good health to enjoy them.

Entrance to our home in Florida

Backyard of our Florida home

Front of our Cleveland home

Great room of our Cleveland home

With the love of my life, 2015

CHAPTER 16

Extra Blessings

Although I must say that many good things happened in our family, I would be remiss if I didn't share with you in this memoir some harrowing accidents that almost culminated in someone's death, and a difficult journey Barb and I took back to my roots, which was important for me to do, but fraught with danger and discomfort. And as I get older, I have come to see that there is no blessing more essential than one's good health. Everything else is secondary.

As I mentioned previously I had an electrocution accident as a teen, which caused me a great deal of suffering and could have resulted in death, but thank goodness, caused no permanent damage. The only permanent damage I suffered from childhood traces to my child imprisonment; such a horrific ordeal, much of my memory of it is buried deeply in my psyche.

In 2014, Doug's son, Jared, who was then a Second Lieutenant in the US Army, had a skydiving accident. He had almost 500 dives to his credit. However, one weekend, while skydiving for pleasure (not on army business), he had an accident and hit the ground at a high speed. This caused him to suffer severe life threatening injuries. He spent three months in a Veteran Affairs Rehab Center where he went through rigorous physical therapy. Thankfully, Jared has since returned to Active Duty in the United States Army, with a full recovery.

I am a Holocaust survivor and have tried to establish a life for my children and grandchildren so they will never have to be in harms way. When my grandson Jared first told me he was joining the United States Army I was very apprehensive to give him my blessing. However, I have grown to appreciate, and become very happy for his decision.

Currently, Jared is on the road of becoming an Army Ranger, and the first step of becoming an Army Ranger as an officer in the army is graduating the Supreme Leadership Ranger School. Jared graduated Ranger school in June of 2015 and on graduation day he told me, "You were the reason I graduated Grandpa." He also gave me the select honor of pinning on his first "Ranger Tab." I read his Ranger Regiment application, and an excerpt from his letter from intent which read: "It was my grandfather who came to the United States after World War II as a Holocaust survivor, and now lives amongst the upper class that drives

Pinning Ranger insignia on my grandson Jared

my spirit. He could have become complacent and maintained what he had many times, but he knew he could achieve more and give his family the life he dreamed of having. I look at him as my drive to succeed in life."

I am a proud survivor of the Holocaust to see that I have achieved my number one goal in life - to provide a better life my for family than I had growing up.

Our daughter Lisa was a cheerleader at Orange High School. She was very talented and was a cheerleader for them for four years. Both Barb and I were at the game when we had quite a scare. In her senior year, she was on top of the pyramid of girls when she took a fall and received a very severe blow to her head. This is the kind of accident that could have been life changing for her, but we were very fortunate.

My grandson Julian (my daughter Lisa's son) survived a harrowing car crash in 2014 when he was only eighteen years old. He was driving on a major highway in Cleveland and lost control of his car; the car hit a utility pole and wound up in a ditch. Fortunately for him and the little dog he was driving with in a convertible with the top up, they were thrown out of the top and both survived with only minor scrapes and scratches.

I don't take the life of my loved ones for granted. These almost-tragedies remind me daily how fortunate we are and I thank the Almighty for protecting my family.

In case I needed any reminders about what a miracle my life is, in 1988, Barbara and I joined a tour group that flew to Europe and was making several stops. The second to last stop was Budapest, Hungary. We decided to leave the group at that point and rent a car to drive through Hungary and Czechoslovakia. The group was flying on for Yugoslavia but we would return to Budapest and fly home from there.

We rented this beautiful Volvo 740 and it was kind of ostentatious for the countryside that we were to travel in. Our first stop would be the city that I was born in, *Satoraljaujhely*, a six-hour drive from

Budapest. I was last there when I was 9 years old, and I was returning at 53 years of age.

It was of course a very emotional experience for me. I recognized the street where my Grandma's house was still standing, even though it was now a paved street rather the cobblestones of my youth. I drove right up to my grandma's house and told Barb, that's it! I checked the house number and I was correct. After looking around the house I knocked on the door and the person living there, a middle-aged Hungarian wearing a peasant dress, answered it. I explained to her that I lived in the house as a child, and asked if I could look around. She let me look around on the outside and instead of seeing the beautiful orchard that was there when I once lived there, it was just an overgrown yard with a large hole where a bomb fell during the war and had not been filled in after the bomb was removed. She did not invite me into the house.

Before we left the house the lady complained to me that she was paying her rent every month and has been asking them to fix her roof and they do not. She wanted to know if I could do anything about it! I was very happy that I was able to find my Grandmother's house, especially after the experience in my hometown *Michalovce* where I could not find anything standing after 40 years.

We did not stay in town since there were no accommodations. We next attempted to cross the border into Czechoslovakia and drive to the city, *Michalovce* where I lived most of my youth. At the border we were asked for our identifications and since I spoke Hungarian it went very easily. The border guards though were very thorough and frightening, even inspecting under our car with mirrors. One of the guards ordered my wife in Hungarian (which I translated) to open the glove compartment. She tried to convince them there was nothing in it, but I told her, "Just open it!" Finally, they let us cross the border. It was a stark reminder to us that we were no longer in democratic, relatively safe, America.

We got over the border and drove 15 minutes to *Michalovce*, which had become practically unrecognizable to me since most of the old buildings had been replaced with new ones. When we drove into the town I had a hard time recognizing the area since a lot of the buildings were gone and new ones or there instead. Since I was last there in 1948 and this was 1989, 40 years later, it's not surprising that the town was not the same place of my youth. The main street where my father had a gas station, and the street off of the main Street where our home was looked entirely different, replaced with a traffic circle! We parked the car and started walking, looking for landmarks that I would remember. I did locate were the temple used to be, but the temple was gone. The chapel was still there, but now being used as a warehouse. The yard I played soccer in next to the chapel had disappeared as well.

I had a very heavy heart when I thought about how the people of this town had treated me in my youth. The two areas where I had lived no longer existed, and that was very disappointing. This was not a happy visit for me. The fear of being a Jew in this city was still in me and I was afraid to ask anyone there about the history of the buildings now standing where the old once stood. I froze and my heart pounded. I did not want anyone to know I was Jewish from my past experience with them.

We were going to spend the night in this town but changed our mind when I visited the only hotel there and the bathroom was, shall we say it nicely - very unacceptable (translation, disgusting!) We continued our travels to the next town, *Kosice*, which was a much larger city where my father used to take the bus from *Michalovce* when he went to work.

On the way there I had remembered stories that my dad had told me about a huge battle that took place in this area where both Russians and Germans were buried three deep in the ground. Sure enough we came to a monument with other remembrances and writings commemorating this battle.

When we arrived in the city of *Kosice* we found a more decent hotel and checked in. We had to give them our passport, which was frightening to us. When we asked about our car, they told us we could park in the basement under the hotel. When we drove the car to the designated parking area, it was three stories down with machinery and beat trucks sitting there. This was not ideal, and unnerved us.

Finally, this robust lady with all kinds of keys on her belt told us where to park the car. She directed us to the basement entrance of the hotel. While driving down to the third level of the basement, passing on the way many farm machinery and tractors, she indicated where we should park. Barb was very concerned and said to me we will never get out of here. Finally the lady motioned for us to get out of the car and directed us to a nearby elevator. When she opened the elevator with one of the keys from the keys on her belt the elevator door opened revealing the inside to barely fit the three of us. We got to our room and everything worked out okay.

About twelve years ago I developed a pain in my right arm and chest, which of course raised the heart attack alarm bells. I was admitted to the hospital and the doctors implanted two stents in my almost ninety percent clogged arteries. I was very fortunate to be diagnosed and treated before the kind of heart attack that could have ended my life. When I was diagnosed in Florida, I asked if I could have the procedure done in Cleveland. He talked to my doctor in Cleveland and I had the procedure done there. This surgery enabled me to get a new life. I was able to play tennis without the labored breathing that I previously had.

They say that a couple in a long marriage, like Barb and me, come to be as one person. Well, Barb and I both recently required back surgeries with rods and screws placed in our backs! She had basically the same surgery as me. I had it done in Florida on emergency basis in April 2014 because of the severe pain I was having. Barb had it done only a few months later, in August 2014 in Cleveland. Barb has recovered nicely and even gone back to playing golf. My recovery was also going well enough that I was able to resume playing golf. But this past summer, I hurt my back again and have been hurting ever since. I went to see my surgeon who, through x-rays and an MRI concluded that I have a pinched nerve, which can be treated with shots to the spine. I scheduled an appointment to have that done, and we are currently in process.

A few months after my back surgery, while I was basically still recovering from that ordeal, my urologist informed me that I had prostate cancer. He recommended radiation treatment, which meant that I needed to receive forty-four radiation treatments. I finished the treatments in February 2014. The treatments were successful and to date, almost two years later, I am cancer free. The treatments lasted about three month and were not debilitating. I basically went on with my normal life. Then, in 2016, my aching back flared up again and required another surgery, which thankfully, I have seen good results from, after some weeks of rehabilitation and recovery.

One might read this last couple of paragraphs of my recent medical maladies and wonder why I include them in a chapter entitled "extra blessings." Well, it's all how you look at it, isn't it?

I was treated for major heart disease before having a fatal heart attack.

Barb and I both recovered from major back surgery and there is effective treatment for my current back pain.

Radiation treatment cured my cancer.

And honestly, to know that my wife, children and grandchildren are currently in good health gives me no measure of gratitude.

So really, what else could I do but include this discussion of medical maladies in a chapter focused on blessings?

We are all familiar with the notion of looking at the glass as half-full or half-empty. I have been open about my struggles with health from time to time in my life, which roots back to my tumultuous childhood, and the loss of my dear mother. But if there was one idea above all else that I would want to leave my children and grandchildren with, it is this:

There are many obstacles in most people's lives. None of us get through life without challenges. Yes, perhaps my imprisonment and becoming an orphan is more extreme than most, but every human being will face tests, and difficult times. This is what I know: No matter what life hands you, the cliché is true – you have a choice about whether to make lemons or lemonade out of it. You can always take positive steps to make an otherwise painful experience better. Success in life isn't really what is given to you – it's what you make out of your circumstances. And you always have this choice: focus on the blessings. An attitude of gratitude, a strong loving marriage to a life-partner, a family life shaped by Jewish traditions, and good loyal friends will take you far in life. And don't forget to have fun along the way.

Olivia carries on Grandma's tradition of challah baking

Grandchildren enjoying the hot tub- Sammy, Zak, Ally, and Jared

Barbara with 5 of 6 grandchildren. Olivia the youngest has not arrived yet

Sammy and Jared

Grandchild Jared went on to play in high school

Jared's graduation as a Ranger, with Doug, Sammy, and Ilene

Jared skydiving

Jared takes pics while sky diving of his sister and instructor

Jared in one of his 500 jumps

Grandson Jared receiving his commission as 2nd lieutenant

Doug and family at the Western Wall

Jared and his father Doug

Jared and Doug at the Western Wall

Like two windup toys, Sammy and Zak

Sammy in early equestrian training

Samantha gathering ribbons and our daughter Lisa's shower

Doug, Jared, Ilene, and Samantha

Our granddaughter Samantha equestrian jumping

Olivia Jared Zak Sammy

Aly and Zak

Aly and Zak

Aly and Zak

Lee on whale with Zak and Aly in our pool

Alyson the actress!

Alyson in the Sound of Music

Granddaughter Aly, as Annie

Alyson (Annie) with her grandparents

Lee and wife Barbara with Aly and Zak

Granddaughter Alyson's wedding- Les, Barb, Aeron, Aly, Barb, Lee, Zak

2002, All of our grandchildren

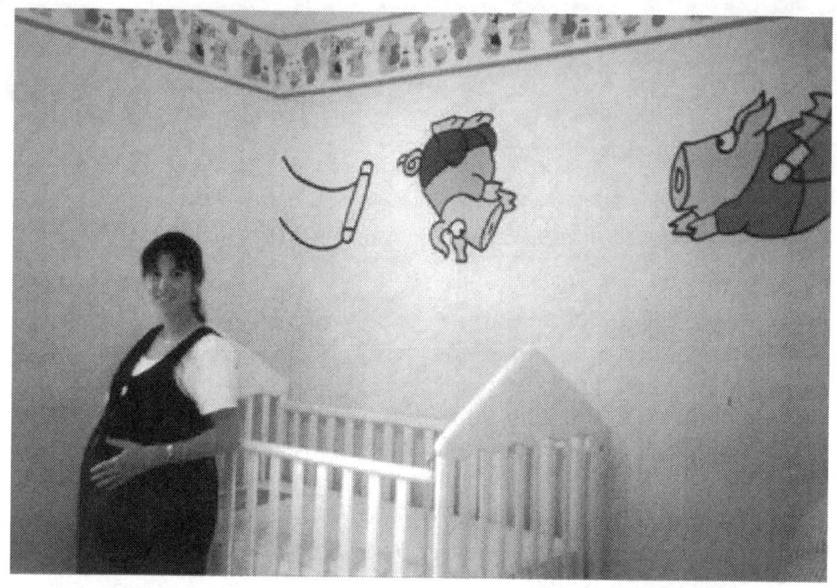

Daughter Lisa pregnant with Julian, wall mural painted by her

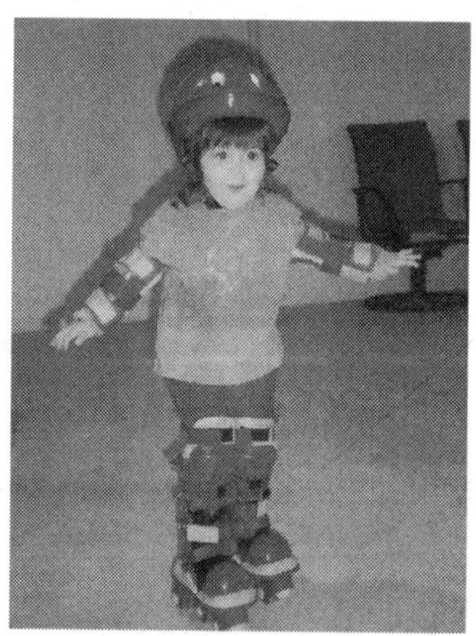

Olivia on skates

Julian, budding artist

Grandpa having dinner in Florida with Julian and Olivia

Julian, Lisa, Shelby, and Olivia

Olivia, bottom right, in Peter Pan

Olivia with mom and dad

Grandchildren, Olivia and Julian

Olivia singer in Orange school band
with mother and friend Zak

Olivia in costume

Granddaughter Olivia receiving National Honor Society certificate

Olivia as Annie

Grandson Julian is proud of the fish he caught!

Grandson Julian's development

Paying respects with Julian to my in-laws

Three generations - Barb, Lisa, and Olivia

Three generations at a soccer game - me, Lee, and Zak

Zak resting on a soccer ball

Grandson Zak with his mom and grandparents

Grandson Zak, me and son Lee

My great-granddaughter Lilah Bea at 8 months

Lee's family

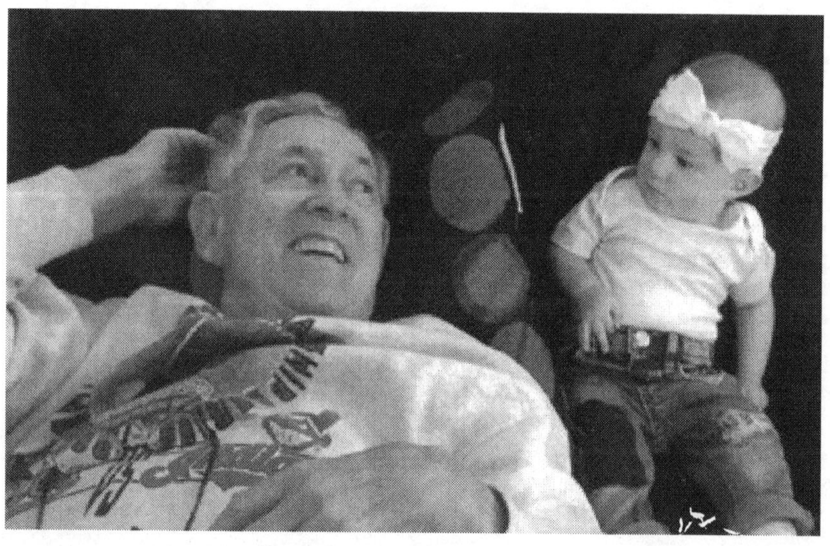

She makes me feel young again!

Lilah visits with grandpa

Aeron and Alyson with Lilah Bea

CHAPTER 17

Friends

My golf buddies, Harvey, Allen, and Jeff

Barb's bridge group

Mel and Marsha Bram

Bob and Sue Wyman

Friends Leanne, Fran, Elaine, Mayryka

Lost a good friend, Jerry Spevak

Friends at the pool

Friends- Sue Wynman, Sandy Babbush, Nancy Katz, and Norma Markowitz

Dinner at Polo Club with friends

Friends and neighbors- Marsha, Pat, Barb, Hedy, and Charlotte

Barb with friend Jacqui

Friends Chris, Carole, Barb, Sue, Marie, and Nancy

Dinner in the kitchen of Oakwood country club,
friends Stanley and Fran Palevsky

Friends from Cleveland and Florida-
David and Jacqui Roseman, Joanne and Larry Adelman

Howard, best man at our wedding

Barb with friends Marie Swain and Sue Rubin

Florida Gin card group-
Sandy Felinger, Larry Adelman, me, Dennis Mormayer, David Roseman

Three members of Monday night Gin group-
Me with Larry Adelman and Ed Friedman

Dr. Marty Markowitz, Stan Davis and me

Stan Davis choking me with onlooker Bob Zelvy

My dear friend Stan, unfortunately no longer with us

*Dr. Jerry and Elaine Weinberg, Bill and Fran Smylie,
Mort and Maryke Weisberg*

Celebrating their daughter's wedding with Stanley and Carole

Carol Davis, me and Barb, Mort Weisberg

We were all married on Sept. 15, 1957
The Mecklers, Dworkins & Barb and I. Celebrating 55th Anniversary

Dr. Jerry Weinberg (Deceased) was an OBGYN and loved children.
Here with Samantha

Dinner at the Polo Club with Matt and Ellen Siegel

Dinner at the Rosemans, Bert Larry, Jim, Don, Dave, and Marty

Friends

Friends

Friends

Friends

Barbara's high school mates

CHAPTER 18

Extended Family

My father and me

Ervin on left and I going to kindergarten 1941

1963, Ervin and me in Los Angeles

Les and Ervin, 2012 (compare to pic from kindergarten in 1942!)

1989 Israel, Barb, Aunt Honor and me

My Aunt Honor, her daughter Nechama, and her children

My Aunt Bosze at Lisa's wedding

My brother Dr. Marvin Friedman
and his wife Ann

My brother Marv and I

Marv's 60th with his wife and two daughters

Marv and I, in our younger years

Marv and I riding a go-kart

Celebrating my 70th birthday with Barb, Ann, and Marv

Cousin Peter and me in Los Angeles

Visiting cousin Edit and her husband Dov in Israel

Seated cousin Trudy, Herbie, me and my brother Marvin

Front cousin Herbie, his sister Trudy and her husband Dr. Robert Licht, their son Dr. Alan Licht and his wife

Cousin Peter, his wife Judy, me and Aunt Bosze

Cousin Nechama, husband and children in Israel

Cousin Herbie and his wife Judy with Barb,
on a visit from California in their motor home

Visiting my cousins in Israel

Cousin Candy and husband Sal

My three living first cousins mother's side, Les, Nechama, and Peter

Cousin Stacy with her husband Dr. Bob Portnoy

Jason and Lauren's wedding in Connecticut

Cousins at Jason and Lauren's wedding in Connecticut

Daughter Lisa with cousins at Connecticut reunion

Connecticut reunion, Olivia center front with cousins

My second cousins Alan and Mark whom I babysat for

My father-in-law and me

Daughter-in-law Ilene and her father Harvey Dick

My father and his wife Cecilia

My son-in-law Shelby, and his father

Daughter in law Barbara with her father Bernie

Barbara's niece Halle and nephew Robb

Marlene and her father

The Friedman family

Barb's sister Marlene, her daughter Halle with her husband Dan, Jake, Ellie, twins Ari, Ryan

Dr. Robert and Cheryl Newman

My niece Susan's bat mitzvah in California

The Gelfands- Herman (brother of Julius), Herbie (cousin to Julius), Hymie (cousin to Julius), and Julius, my father-in-law

Uncle Herman and Barbara

My cousin Ervin's son, a career pilot and retired officer

Margie
304-669-5582

10/27 -
Eli dinner
6:30